PRESENTED TO:

_____

BY:

_____

DATE:

_____

07 06 05 04 03   10 9 8 7 6 5 4 3 2 1

Be Patient, God Isn't Finished with Me Yet
ISBN 1-56292-916-X
Copyright © 2003 by Honor Books,
An Imprint of Cook Communications Ministries
P.O. Box 55388
Tulsa, Oklahoma 74155

Written and compiled by Vicki Kuyper, Colorado Springs, CO

BE PATIENT,
GOD ISN'T FINISHED
WITH ME YET

by

A Fellow Traveler on the Road of Life

CONTENTS

CHAPTER 1

We learn wisdom from failure

much more than from success.

We often discover what will do,

by finding out what will not do,

and probably he who never made a mistake

never made a discovery.

SAMUEL SMILES

THE GOOD NEWS:
YOU'RE STILL UNDER CONSTRUCTION

uilding a house begins with an idea, then a formal plan. Just add a foundation, some wood, nails, drywall, wiring, plumbing, insulation, carpeting, light fixtures, counters, doors, windows, paint, and roofing materials, along with a host of permits and inspections, some professional expertise, months of labor, and POOF. You have a house. Kinda. But if it takes all of that just to build a house, imagine what it takes to build a human life.

Luckily, God has taken care of the hard part. He's created a way where one cell turns into two, then four, then eight, and on and on. In nine months' time, there is what looks like a finished product—at least a miniature version of the finished product. But it can't yet walk or talk. Even its discernment over what's edible and what's not is rather questionable at times. It is moody and self-centered, not to mention noisy. It keeps odd hours and demands more attention than a prima donna on a world tour.

Most people would agree that babies are a work in progress. They're not quite finished yet. We've come to expect that they take a bit of time and training. They still need to grow tall enough so that their feet can reach the accelerator on an SUV, strong enough to carry a full basket of laundry, and smart enough to operate a VCR. But once a baby—say you, for instance—has reached adulthood, we assume that the "building" is pretty much over. Now you're a grown-up. You're responsible. You're finally who you were always meant to be. Well, kinda. . . .

Human life develops more like a novel than a housing project. Instead of following a step-by-step plan where identical houses can be built over and over again, the life of every individual is written page by page as each day goes by. There are plenty of twists and turns, and perceived villains and heroes along the way. You never know what's going to happen next. What may begin as a tragedy may end up as a heroic epic, or vice versa.

And while some babies may look alike to everyone but their parents, the stories of their lives will never be identical—even if they're twins. Tract homes may be popular with developers, but individuals are Heaven's Master Plan.

Just as a story cannot truly be told unless you tell it from beginning to end, a life cannot be judged from somewhere in the middle. You and I continue to be works in progress. That means our expectations of ourselves and others need to take into account the fact that God is not finished with us yet. Today, we may be selfish, disorganized, and stingy. But that doesn't mean we will always be. It also doesn't take into account that perhaps last year we were pig-headed, narrow-minded, and lacking in social skills. People change. And as they do, so do their stories.

What does your story look like right now? Do you look at how far you've come or how far you have to go? Are other people in your life trying to edit your story for you? Do you try to portray one type of character to the world, in order to cover quite a different scenario going on beneath the surface? Do you want to rewrite certain chapters of your life? Or do you wish you could rip up the story you have and begin again?

This book is about change; the you and me we are changing into—and out of—each and every day. It is also about hope. The hope of filling your story with wonder, beauty, love, and joy; even when the world around you seems to be writing a tragic tale. It may sound impossible. But with God, the impossible happens every day. Just look at what He can do with one simple cell.

CHAPTER 2

Our confidence in Christ . . . awakens us,

urges us on, and makes us active in

living righteous lives and doing good.

There is no self-confidence to compare with this.

ULRICH ZWINGLI

It's Not Really All about Me

ats have a certain way of looking at the world that the majority of us humans seem determined to emulate. Cats are rather docile, and friendly enough to those around them—when it's convenient and pleases them. They purr when they're pampered. They scratch when they're annoyed. They spend a lot of time grooming themselves and lying in the sun napping. In other words, they do whatever feels good right now. Cats really don't care who you are. They only care about what you can do for them.

If cats had to have a statement of purpose, it would be this: It's all about me. Now, before we go too far, let's get one thing straight: I like cats. Really. I'm not the kind of person who puts a bumper sticker on my car that reads, "So many cats, so few recipes." Snoozy and Pickle Wheezer were two of my closest friends growing up, and both of them were of the feline persuasion. But just because I think cats make nice pets doesn't mean I look up to them as role models.

Cats lack one very important human quality. They do not know how to put others before themselves. Have you ever seen two tabbies reach the food bowl at the same time, and then one of them graciously gestures, "By all means, after you"? Cats are cats. But God created you and me differently. We have the ability to sacrifice our own time, and to offer comfort and our resources to help others. Then why does it feel so natural to follow the cat philosophy of "It's all about me"? The truth is, old habits are hard to break. But the even more exciting truth is that God can break even the power old habits exert in our lives. That's the truth we need to pursue.

When we first came into this world, we had a lot in common with cats. After all, babies demand that their needs be met before anyone else's. They'll put anything into their mouths. They spend most of their days sleeping. And they never clean up their own messes. But the Bible has something to say about what should happen after that. First Corinthians 13:10 says that when we were children, we spoke and thought and reasoned like children do. But when we grow up by seeking God and allowing Him freely into our lives, we put away childish things.

Let's face it. The world is not our litter box. It's time we put away our feline tendencies and grow up. The first step involves changing our philosophy of life—shifting our perspective. It's not "all about me." It's "all about what God wants to do through me."

At this point, most people begin panicking. They're afraid they may be missing God's will in their lives. What if He wants them to be missionaries in some country they can't even pronounce or give up their lucrative careers to become church janitors? You know what? He might. But chances are, He's more concerned with who we are becoming than what cities we're living in or what our resumés look like.

First and foremost, He's concerned about how we're growing. Are we maturing or refusing to leave the safety of our cribs? If we compare ourselves with where we were last year, have we changed for the better? As we age, do we have fewer catlike tendencies? Or are we spending more of our time, money, and attention pampering ourselves than ever before?

We may not be able to teach an old cat, or a young cat for that matter, new tricks. But God has made human beings very adaptable. We choose who, or what, is going to be the center of our lives. If we always have to have our own way, have to be first, grab the biggest piece, and cannot handle being inconvenienced for the sake of others, do we really want to become who God created us to be? Or is our own agenda the real bottom line?

The next time a cat crosses your path, why not use it as a reminder to check where your true priorities lie? Ask yourself, "Today, am I living life as if it is only all about me?"

CHAPTER 3

God works powerfully,
but for the most part gently and gradually.

JOHN NEWTON

EVEN HEROES TRIP OVER THEIR CAPES ONCE IN AWHILE

hink back. For some of you it may be way back. Remember taking a class in English literature? What do you remember most? (Don't worry. This won't involve a grade.) One thing I remember is that all heroes had something in common. They all had a fatal flaw. Achilles had his heel. Superman had kryptonite. David had Bathsheba.

Can you name your fatal flaw? I have to admit, my first response to this question is, "You want me to name only ONE?" But if I had to narrow down my list, fear would rise to the top. Although that's a rather general weakness, fear has reared its ugly head in many different ways throughout my life. I'm afraid of failure. Afraid of what people think. Afraid of calling someone I don't know on the telephone. Sounds ridiculous, right?

Although hesitating to call and order pizza may not be a life-or-death situation, what if I had to call 911?

The good news is that I've not only been aware of my fears, but have been facing them head-on for the last several years. So when the day came when I did have to call for an ambulance, I didn't hesitate. I dialed.

That's what dealing with weakness is all about. It's acknowledging your weakness and then facing it head-on. Not knowing your fatal flaw is like spending your life walking through a mine field. You never know when something's going to blow up in your face. But knowing where your weaknesses lie is like having a map that tells you where every mine is buried. Instead of being taken by surprise, it gives you choices. You can either avoid the land mines or disarm them.

Suppose one of your fatal flaws is your addiction to doughnuts. This weakness may not destroy your life, but it's not doing your waistline or cholesterol count any favors. But, suppose you drive past the doughnut shop every day on the way to work. The first thing you need to do is choose an alternate route! Why put yourself into a situation where you know you're likely to fail? The same advice holds true whether you find yourself drawn to pornography on the Internet or too many beers after work. Stay away from the computer, and don't fill the fridge with beer.

But that's just the first step. The roots of most weaknesses have to be faced head-on. They have to be disarmed. Just ignoring weaknesses won't make them go away. What it does is set you up for defeat. Whether it's through counseling, self-help programs, or prayer with an accountability partner, learning to tackle your weaknesses is like practicing defensive driving. You're ready no matter what lies ahead.

Just remember that you're not alone. All of the great heroes in literature, and life, have an area of weakness that has the potential to bring them to their knees. Maybe that's just the way God planned it. Our weaknesses remind us that we're human, not divine. They force us to lean on Someone larger than ourselves. They keep us humble.

Take a lesson from the Amish. Well known for their beautiful and skillfully made quilts, the Amish put a "flaw" in every quilt they make. They do this on purpose to remind the artist, and those who see each masterpiece, that only God is perfect. Uncovering, admitting, and facing areas of weakness in your life not only adds depth and beauty to the personal work of art God is creating in you, but helps set free the true hero you're meant to be.

CHAPTER 4

Are you in earnest? Seize this very minute!

What you can do, or dream you can, begin it.

Boldness has genius, power and magic in it.

Only engage, and then the mind grows heated.

Begin and then the work will be completed.

JOHANN WOLFGANG GOETHE

Never Put Off till Tomorrow What You Should Have Done Yesterday

I did a really stupid thing. Then I did another stupid thing. First, I didn't thoroughly read the directions on my application for passport renewal—until after I'd mailed it. I'd breezed over the line that read, "Although the second page requires no data from the applicant, it contains important information regarding official legal statements. It should be read before completing the form and MUST be submitted with the completed first page." Oops. I'd only put the first page into the envelope. That was my first "stupid thing."

Once I realized what I'd done, or not done, I panicked. I was leaving for Turkey in eight weeks. The passport office had said my new passport would take four to six weeks to arrive. If I botched my application, there was a chance my passport wouldn't be back in my anxious little hands until AFTER the plane took off. My panic grew to gargantuan proportions.

That's when I noticed a phone number—at $1.05 a minute—where I could check on the status of my passport. I'd call them up, explain what an idiot I'd been, and then see what I needed to do to rectify the situation. Simple enough. Except, remember my irrational fear of the phone? So I decided that it was pointless to call right away. After all, my incomplete application had to travel from Colorado to Pennsylvania through the postal service. I'd wait a few days until it got there. Why do it right now? That was my second "stupid thing."

The longer I waited, the dumber I felt—and the more desperate. In my mind, I pictured myself waving good-bye to my husband as he boarded the plane to Istanbul, alone. Every night I went to sleep with my stomach in knots. But I still didn't call.

Until one morning, when God and I had a long chat about what was the worst thing that could happen. The operator could laugh uncontrollably at my irresponsibility, or give me a lecture on the importance of reading directions thoroughly before attempting anything as monumental as a passport renewal. Neither were life-or-death situations. I picked up the receiver, took a deep breath, and made the call. Imagine my surprise when I found out that my passport had gone through without a hitch and was already on its way back to me. I felt great! And stupid. I had let two weeks go by with my stomach tied up in knots. What a waste.

That's exactly what procrastination is. A waste. A waste of time and energy. A source of stress and anxiety. Why do we do it? Because for some reason our confused little minds think that if we do something later, it won't be as unpleasant, difficult, or time-consuming as if we buckled down and got it done now.

Why not save that twenty-page report until the night before it's due? You work best under pressure, right? Why finish your taxes before April 15? The government wouldn't have created the extension unless it was to your benefit to use it, right? Why apologize right now for that thoughtless comment you made over lunch? It's better to wait until your friend is in a better mood and you're feeling more eloquent, right? Wrong. The longer we wait, the harder it gets.

Once a pattern of procrastination has developed in our lives, the best way to break it is to take at least one step forward every day. That begins with making a list. Write down everything you've been putting off, from apologizing to your next-door neighbor, to getting the carpets cleaned. It may be overwhelming to look at, but it's a step in the right direction.

Sort the list into two categories: Must and Should. Under "Must," list things that will have grave consequences if put off much longer. This includes anything that might damage a relationship or put your job or health in jeopardy. Under "Should," list things that have less grave consequences, such as changing the oil in the car or sending out Christmas cards.

Five days a week, do one thing on your *Must* List. On the sixth day do one on your *Should* List. Then take a day off and start all over again. If something takes more than one day to complete, spend some time on it every day until it is completed. Then you can cross it off and go on to the next thing on the list. If your lists are overly long, move some things from your *Should* List to your *Must* List as time goes by.

Just don't give up. Procrastination never accomplished anything other than making life more miserable.

Chapter 5

*Oh, great Father, never let me
judge another man until I have
walked in his moccasins
for two weeks.*

NATIVE AMERICAN PRAYER

Try Walking a Mile in Someone Else's Loafers

B umper to bumper, the line of cars snaked its way over the mountain pass. Every corner I turned gave me a better view of just how far the oncoming traffic was backed up. The end was nowhere in sight. Luckily I was driving the opposite direction. The traffic on my side of the highway was going its usual ten miles over the speed limit, while the cars to my left were almost at a standstill. The slower they went, the more free I felt. I was on the right side. I was lucky. I was blessed.

"You know, Mom," my daughter commented from the passenger seat, "I bet that somewhere in all those cars is a kid who really needs to go to the bathroom."

Though my daughter is a teenager, she hasn't lost touch with the little kid she was not so long ago. She instantly empathized with all the kids stuck in those slow-moving cars. My empathy only took me from "poor them" to "lucky me." Hers put her right there in the back seat with every kid on the way down the mountain who was desperately praying for a restroom. How far does your empathy take you?

When you pick up the newspaper and see photos of flood victims in a country somewhere that you couldn't even locate on a map, do you pause? Or do you note the headline and then quickly turn to the business section to see if the NASDAQ is moving in your portfolio's favor? When you see someone sleeping on a bench in a city park, covered only with a tattered newspaper, do you first ask yourself, "I wonder when was the last time he took a shower?" or "I wonder when was the last time he had a hot meal?" Can you put yourself in his shoes? Or do you find the very thought repulsive? Do you find it an exercise in futility because, after all, you're not in his shoes? You're in those great leather pumps you just got on sale to go with your new suit.

But how hard would it really be to find yourself on that park bench, or in that newspaper photo searching desperately for your children throughout a refuge camp? Change your parents, your race, your economic status. Lose your job, your spouse, your mental health. Spend your childhood on the other side of the world, in an orphanage, infected with AIDS. It's amazing how quickly the story of your life could change.

Empathy can take you places that frequent flyer miles never could. But just getting there is worthless if it does nothing to change your heart. Empathy doesn't change the world. Only love can do that. That's because love can't just sit by and watch. Empathy can cry over newspaper headlines, but only love feels the need to do anything about it.

Imagine how differently you would read the newspaper if the front-page photo was of your next door neighbor searching for her lost child. Or picture what you would do if that homeless person you found in the park turned out to be your best friend. Chances are you wouldn't dream of just walking away.

Now you and I can't save the world. That's God's job. But learning to put ourselves in others' shoes, whether our spouse's, our children's, our best friend's, our worst enemy's, or a total stranger's, is the first step toward really loving them.

Chapter 6

I pray thee, O God,
that I might be beautiful within.

Socrates

BEAUTY LIES BETWEEN A ROCK AND A HARD PLACE

id you ever feel like a geode? You know, those funny round rocks that look like nothing more than a rough, lumpy, gray ball. The surprise is that when you open them up they are filled with delicate, colorful crystals forming intricate shapes and beautiful patterns. They prove true the proverb that says, "You can't judge a book (or a rock) by its cover."

But that proverb is just the opposite of the message that most of us have been taught in real life. That message goes something like this: What you see is what you get! In other words, what people look like on the outside determines their worth. How kind has that mindset been to you throughout the years?

If you're one of the few people born with supermodel genes, they may have opened a few doors for you along the way. They may have helped attract your first boyfriend or get you elected prom queen. But they may also have led some people to believe that you were nothing more than a pretty face. They may have intimidated others, keeping them from ever attempting to get to know you.

And for the rest of the world, the ones whose faces so often get lost in the crowd, the way you look on the outside may have kept people at arm's length, as well. It may have relegated you to the category of ordinary. It may even have been a source of ridicule or embarrassment.

But no matter whether you're drop-dead gorgeous or as plain as a plug nickel according to the world's standards of beauty, one fact holds true: What you look like on the outside says nothing about how attractive you are on the inside.

No matter what we look like on the outside, God has hidden something beautiful in each of us. But there's a catch. Just like the geode, this beauty only becomes visible to others once we open up. This may be as simple as speaking honestly with one another, instead of trying to win others over by being who we think they'd like us to be. It may happen when we become vulnerable enough in the presence of others that unbidden tears don't make us hide or crack a joke. Or maybe it takes place when we have the courage to stand up for what we believe in, no matter what others say.

But sometimes God uses difficult situations in life to break us open all at once. Loneliness, grief, pain, injustice, trauma, betrayal—the hammers God uses to crack open our tough exteriors are as varied as the hearts they break. Yet these fissures in the lives we've tried so hard to hold together somehow lead us deeper. They expose us for who we really are. Yes, they can expose our weaknesses, but they also present the opportunity for unexpected beauty to shine through. Traits like courage, perseverance, integrity, peace, and sacrificial love shine brightest when life looks darkest.

That beauty is not lost on those around us. There is something about people who have endured hardship with grace that brings a genuine beauty to their smiles, an inviting warmth to their friendships, and a compelling promise of wisdom to their words. Will you allow God to open you up widely enough so that others can see the beauty He's carefully crafted in your heart?

It isn't always easy. It isn't always comfortable. But it's certainly worthwhile. Not only does it help others discover who you really are, it does the same thing for you. If you've spent your life feeling like a geode, or, even worse, a garden variety rock that looks as ordinary on the inside as it does on the outside, it's time to enjoy the unique beauty you hold. Without you, the world truly would be a less beautiful place.

CHAPTER 7

———— ⌒ ————

Pay every debt as if God wrote the bill.

—————————

RALPH WALDO EMERSON

THE POT AT THE END OF THE RAINBOW ISN'T FILLED WITH GOLD CARDS

I t's Saturday night and the evening news is about to begin. But in those few moments between commercials and current events, a miracle is about to take place. Someone may become a millionaire. As my husband and I watch those little numbered balls roll down the chute, we keep our lucky numbers in mind. And as those balls fall into their slots and reveal the winning combination, my husband and I always give a little combined sigh. "Won again," one of us says with a smile. We made a buck.

Actually, we've never purchased a lottery ticket. And considering that our lucky numbers have never proven to be a winning combination, at least not in any lottery drawing we've ever seen, we consider the dollar we didn't spend as our winnings. So if we haven't spent a dollar on a lottery ticket for every week of our twenty-year marriage, you could say we've earned over $1,000. That beats the winnings of everyone I personally know who's ever played the lottery.

Not that there aren't winners. Consider the man who won $7.5 million in Ohio in 1992.

One of the first things he bought with his winnings was a new house. He was later convicted of aggravated arson after burning the house to the ground. He said that winning the lottery had turned his life into a "living hell."

But we'd be smarter, right? You and I would use our winnings wisely. Or would we? Consider this. Most Americans already earn over $1 million in their lifetimes. Do you feel like a millionaire?

Prosperity is really a matter of attitude, not an amount of money. Remember the lottery winner who burned down his house? Before he won, I bet he believed that winning all of that money would solve his problems. Afterward, he blamed the money he'd won for causing all of his problems.

Money doesn't cause problems. People who fall in love with it do. The tricky part is that to love money, you don't even have to have it. All you have to do is spend your time dreaming about having it, or whatever it can buy. But money is merely a tool. Falling in love with it is like having an affair with your weed eater—not very fulfilling.

How do you love money? Every affair has its own unique twist. It begins with a minor flirtation as a kid when you begin to mistake your wants for your needs. "But Dad, I NEED that computer game." Next comes rationalization. "If I get that game, my computer skills will get better, and then I'll get better grades in school!" It's soon followed by feeling deprived if other people have something you don't. "Kevin's parents bought him that game, and it wasn't even on sale!" But the real clincher comes when you not only HAVE to have something. You have to have it NOW. "But, Dad, that's what credit cards are for!"

Using a credit card kind of feels a bit like having won the lottery. At least for a little while. But it's an illusion. It's like my husband and I seeing our lucky numbers match those on the lottery balls Saturday night, and then running out to spend our expected winnings—without ever having purchased a ticket. It's spending tomorrow's earnings today. But tomorrow never fails to show up—kind of like those credit card statements.

And for what do we sacrifice the future? For stuff. Stuff that's on sale. But when we buy it on credit, we end up paying more than we would have at regular price. Stuff that we think will make us feel better when we are having a rough day. Stuff to make our kids happy because we feel guilty about working all those extra hours to pay off the consolidation loan. Stuff to take care of, to dust, to dry-clean, to fix, to return. Stuff to sell at our next garage sale or give away to charity. Stuff we never needed in the first place.

The amazing thing is that by just living in America we have, in a sense, won the lottery. Most of us actually have what would be classified as disposable income. Much of the rest of the world doesn't have that luxury. Can you begin each day by counting your blessings? Sure you can! And maybe, when that temptation hits to pull out a card to borrow from tomorrow, you'll find strength to walk away—because you realize how much you have already been given.

—◯—

CHAPTER 8

Help thy brother's boat across,
and lo! thine own has reached the shore.

HINDU PROVERB

THE LONE RANGER NEVER WON A FOOTBALL GAME

Water is an amazing thing. We drink it, bathe in it, and ski on it. We can't live without it. But a tiny raindrop seems almost insignificant, something easily discarded with the flick of a windshield wiper. As Mother always said, "A little rain can't hurt you." But when one drop gathers with another, and then another, the power behind what those drops can do as a team makes water one of the most powerful forces on earth—even in the desert.

Did you know that every year more people die from drowning in the desert than from dehydration? Sounds impossible, doesn't it? But when a sudden storm hits, arid ground does not have the capability of soaking up the excess water as quickly as does soil that has been exposed to a more consistent rainfall. This makes even a small cloudburst in desert regions a potential flash flood.

Water can offer a gentle massage in a jacuzzi tub or carve canyons and run power plants. But again, a single drop couldn't do either job on its own. Its power is exerted through a team effort. But once that team is set in motion, it can even work its way through solid rock. In 1969, the flow of water over one of Niagara's three falls was stopped so that rocks could be removed at the base to give it a more dramatic appearance. After a few months, the project was abandoned, because the effort and expense were considered too great. But the 750,000 gallons of water that roar over the falls every second have their own remodeling program. Every year, the edge of Niagara Falls recedes an average of four inches, carving out a deeper niche into the solid rock it travels over. Water succeeded where humans had given up.

It's just a good thing that God did not give each of those individual water droplets a brain. Can you imagine the chaos? "I want to go THIS way!" "Well, that's the wrong way. We're going THIS way!" "I don't need you. I can do this on my own!" "Fine then, why don't you!" Earth would be lucky to have a handful of cooperative drops willing to join together long enough to make a puddle.

Sound familiar? Perhaps you've faced a similar scenario on the job, at home, or even at church. Everyone has their own agenda. No one wants to give an inch. Consequently, whatever you're trying to accomplish can't move forward. Until you agree on a common vision, you're stuck. If a group of people is not even heading in the same direction, how can they expect to make any progress? You're a rogue river without a compass.

Working together effectively as a team begins with a plan. It means matching individuals to the tasks in which they are best suited to succeed. It means listening to others' ideas and being willing to put your own on hold if it's in the group's best interest. It means encouraging one another along the way. And it means sharing the glory of victory when your goal is finally met.

What can be accomplished by a team cannot be equaled by the efforts of an individual—even a determined individual. Try moving a couch, conceiving a child, or playing a piece of music intended for an orchestra. A single violin cannot do justice to Beethoven's *Fifth Symphony*. It's not that the violin is inferior or unimportant. It's just that it's designed to be part of a team. And so are we.

God said in Ephesians 4:4 that we are all one body. That means we were designed to fit together, and to work as a team. To function properly as one body, every part needs to participate. If the lungs decide they're taking the day off, the whole body's in trouble. If one foot rebels against the other, the entire body just goes around in circles.

How well are you working as part of the body? Are you able to ask for help when you need it? Can you work together on a team without being the leader? Do you feel other parts of the body are less important, or more important, than you are? Do you prefer the role of Lone Ranger?

Pulling yourself up by your own bootstraps may be perceived as the motto every American adult should live by. But try doing it sometime. A team effort can mean success. Join your efforts to the efforts of others and change your world!

CHAPTER 9

In youth we learn;

in age we understand.

MARIE EBNER-ESCHENBACH

Today Is the Youngest
You'll Ever Be Again

L ast week I found myself lying on my bedroom carpet for almost an hour. It wasn't that I was exhausted or working hard to get a stubborn stain out of the synthetic fibers. The fact was, I'd reached down to pick up a shoe. Then my hip went out. In serious pain, I fell to the ground and couldn't move.

Right below me, a group of teenagers was having a meeting in my dining room. I debated about what I should do. I was too cheap to call an ambulance. And my pride wouldn't let me yell down to the teens below, "I've fallen and I can't get up!" So I just lay on the floor until a girlfriend showed up an hour later to help me ease myself down the stairs and grab some pain reliever.

I felt it was the beginning of the end. My daughter confirmed that fact just a few days later. I was showing her a bathing suit I'd just purchased on sale. She looked at it with horror. "But, Mom," she said, "It has a skirt!"

"It's not a skirt!" I said adamantly. "It's just a flap!" A flap. Who was I kidding? On a bathing suit, a flap is like a training bra for a skirt. I was watching my youth go down in flames.

Aging is no respecter of persons. It seems as though as soon as we're old enough to know what we want out of life, we're too old to do anything about it. There are some people, like Raquel Welch and Tina Turner, who seem to have hit some kind of aging time warp; but for the rest of us, going over the hill is no pleasure trip.

The message we seem to get from the world and our own egos is, "If God isn't finished with me yet, He'd better hurry, because time is running out!" But God's timing is always perfect. As the book of Ecclesiastes reminds us, there is a season for everything. We can take time to enjoy the season we're in.

Life is a series of seasons: the total dependence of infancy, childhood, adolescence, independence, marriage, parenthood, empty nest, then dependence on others once more. Each individual's seasons may look different. Some people remain single; others marry, but never have children; and still others may have a mental or physical condition that keeps them dependent on others throughout their lives. Some may have a short growing season and die as children. Others may live to see their hundredth birthday. On the outside, there may seem to be no rhyme or reason. But God has a plan. And that plan includes finding joy and wisdom in the seasons He brings your way.

No matter where you find yourself in life, you're in a season of celebration. Yes, celebration! Every age has its struggles and its victories, its restrictions and its privileges. After a mid-life season, aging may not seem to be doing the body any favors; but there is a wisdom and contentment that can take root, bringing with it an understanding of what really matters in life. We spend less time trying to make a name for ourselves and more time enjoying who God has created us to be. We realize that relationships are more important than revenue. We accept that our lives on this earth will one day come to an end. And we anticipate what eternity will be like. Of course, those are only generalizations. Some people seem to grow older without growing wiser. They've missed learning from, and enjoying, the seasons they've passed along the way.

Don't let the age on your driver's license determine your season in life. As I mentioned before, everyone's growing seasons look a bit different. What do you have to celebrate about the season you're in right now? What are you looking forward to in the season to come? Go on now—live your life in a way that reflects your answers.

CHAPTER 10

He who cannot forgive

breaks the bridge over which

he himself must pass.

GEORGE HERBERT

KEEP YOUR FAMILY TIES TANGLE-FREE

W hat's a family worth? It's hard to believe that what some feel is merely "luck of the draw" can become one of our strongest relational foundations in life. It can also become one of our greatest heartaches. Just look at the soap operas. Renaldo's mother is having an affair with his best friend. Renaldo's sister is taking him to court because he embezzled funds from her trust account. Renaldo's wife has hired a private eye to investigate her ex-husband who she believes is stalking their family. And Renaldo's children—well, they haven't spoken to him for over two seasons now.

But that's fiction, right? One can only hope. But the truth is that the melodrama of some real-life families often plays out more like a bad television script than what's found on daytime TV. How does it get that way? It usually begins with one tangle at a time; one sharp word heaped on one betrayal, sideswiped by one unvoiced apology, and topped off by one selfish act—just to mention a few of the countless possibilities.

Family ties do not begin as two unencumbered pieces of string coming together to make a pleasing bow. They are more like a tapestry, woven tightly over time. They can be a beautiful work of art, or a collage of tattered hearts. And sometimes, we're born right into the middle of that tangled, mixed-up mess.

It's not our fault, but here we are. So, what do we do? First, we need to remember that there is no knot so complex that God cannot untangle it. Then we need to do our part in not pulling it any tighter. Romans 12:18 says that as far as it depends on us, we should live in peace with one another. That includes living in peace with those we're related to, by marriage or blood.

Doing that takes work. We need to keep the lines of communication open. We need to apologize for our part in any problem. We need to make an effort to love those who may not be easily lovable. We need to forgive and ask for forgiveness. We need to be willing to go out of our way for someone who may not deserve it. We need to recognize that everyone is imperfect, and that includes us. We need to do the hard work of getting along together. We need to find out what love really means.

That takes us straight back to God. Loving imperfect people is a tough job. Just ask God. But for some reason, God designed every one of us to be born into families, instead of just bursting into life spontaneously, ready to face the world on our own. Our families may look different. Our childhood experiences may be diverse. But the call of God to love one another remains the same.

Love is a gift that's chosen carefully. Sometimes love will involve letting others lean on us for a while. Other times it may mean moving far enough away so they can learn to stand alone. The better we know someone, the better we'll be at choosing just the right way to share our love. One way to get a deeper, broader view of love in action is to read the Bible. How God treated people, imperfect people, throughout the Gospels will help expand our own personal definition of love.

Acting on what we know we should do isn't always easy. But God never said love would be easy. He only said it was the right thing to do and that He would make it possible for us to do what seems impossible. And that's a promise. The steps of love you take will untangle ties that have been in knots for years, even the ones inside you.

Unfortunately, you may find yourself in a family that has no desire to get out of the knot they've gotten themselves into. You can do all the right things, but the final result isn't in your hands. It isn't even in God's. That's because having free will means that individuals make their own choices, both good and bad. But you're part of a bigger family than the one you were born into, adopted into, or married into. First, and foremost, you're a child of God. And your Heavenly Father is the only perfectly functional parent anyone can have. Why not take a moment to make the shift? Let Him love you and be the family you need. He won't let you down.

CHAPTER 11

All I have seen teaches me to trust

the Creator for all I have not seen.

RALPH WALDO EMERSON

It Takes Faith to Fly a Kite

Did you ever build a kite as a kid? You'd take a couple of pieces of balsa wood, some paper, glue, and string. Then you'd pray for a breeze. But did you ever think about how much faith it took to run through a field, dragging your fragile creation behind you?

Some days the kite took off in a matter of minutes, dipping and darting as the wind pulled it up into the sky. Other times, no matter how fast you ran or how high you tried to jump, the kite continued to drag along behind you, until you finally gave up and went inside. Your success depended on something you couldn't control—something you couldn't even see. But you still believed it was there. You'd seen what the wind could do before. You had faith it would happen again.

The book of Hebrews, chapter 11, talks about the essence of faith. It explains that what is done in faith gives evidence to what cannot be seen. Running through the field trying to launch a kite gives evidence that there's something you're trusting in other than your own strength to get that kite up into the air. How much you trust in the power of the wind depends on three things: what others have told you about it, your experience with it, and how much you're willing to risk trusting something you cannot see.

Your first step of faith in flying a kite was trusting in what others said the wind could do. You may have read a book, seen a kite on TV, learned about wind power in school, or watched as friends ran through the field with a kites of their own. Once you judged that your sources were reliable, things got a little more personal.

You may have had experience with wind in the past. You felt it blow against your face in a storm. You saw it whip leaves down the street on a fall day. You saw video of a hurricane picking up a trailer home. Certainly, in your experience, wind seems strong enough to carry a little balsa wood and paper through the sky.

You may believe in the wind. But until you trust the wind with your precious kite, you don't have faith in it. Faith involves action.

You may believe that spring will come again next year. But planting your tulip bulbs in the fall is more than belief. It's an act of faith. You're acting as though something will happen before it actually has. You're putting your trust in something you cannot see.

Do you believe in God? If so, does what you believe have any effect on your life? We can believe in God and not have faith in Him. We may have heard what others have said about Him. We may have examined our own experience as to whether He really is who He says He is. But until we risk doing something where we have to trust Him, our faith is not real. It's just a theory we ponder, a philosophy we agree with.

Faith only grows through exercise. We may risk only small things—at first. "I'll risk wasting a few moments of time in prayer on the off-chance that God will really answer." But as we experience more of God's power in our lives, our faith—and willingness to risk—will grow. "I know this job doesn't pay as much as the one I have now, but I'm willing to risk it because I believe it's where God wants me to be." Our picture of God is as big as our faith.

But what happens on the day that the wind isn't there—the day that our kites refuse to fly? Some days it feels as though God's doing the same thing as the wind—taking a day off. We may pray about things that don't change right away. Faith doesn't give up when God's answer or timing isn't the same as our own. It doesn't put the kite in the closet and forget about it. Faith goes out into the field, trusting that God will show up when it's time for that kite to fly. Faith acts in confidence because it knows who God really is.

Taking time every day to talk with God about your life strengthens your faith as He reveals His true self to you. The stronger your faith, the more you can view problems as opportunities for Him to show you just what He can do—His way. You'll find yourself bravely buying the biggest ball of kite string you can find to wait patiently for just the right breeze to lift your kite above the fences that seem to stand in the way.

CHAPTER 12

Tell God all that is in your heart,

as one unloads one's heart to a dear friend.

FRANCOIS DE FÉNELON

REFLECTION IS MORE THAN
YOUR FACE IN THE MIRROR

R emember the movie *Groundhog Day?* Bill Murray lives the same day over and over again until he gets his part right. Wouldn't that be nice? Forget about those angry words that slipped out before you could stop them. Next time around you'll see the problem coming and hold your tongue. Or how about that pothole in the highway you hit going 75 miles per hour and blew your tire? Next time you'll slow down or just avoid it altogether. And if you get to the end of your life and discover that, yes, there really is a God, don't despair. You'll know better next time around and act accordingly.

But real life doesn't work that way. Or does it? It's true, we only get one shot at every day. One shot at choosing how to live our lives. We cannot change the past, but we can learn from it. And isn't that exactly what's happening in *Groundhog Day?*

As the old saying goes, "Those who ignore the past are doomed to repeat it." But to learn from our mistakes, we need to stop long enough to recognize that we've made them. Then we need to decide how we are going to avoid them in the future.

Every morning, as we get ready to face the day, we spend a few moments in front of the mirror. We check our reflection to make sure we look presentable. We may brush our hair, shave our whiskers, or cover up those unsightly blemishes. Although we may feel better after we're all put together, our efforts have really been for other people, not ourselves. If we don't know that our hair is sticking up like Medusa's twin sister or that we have a piece of spinach blacking out one of our teeth like a modern-day pirate, we feel fine. It's only after we discover that others have seen us looking less than our best that embarrassment hits. That's when we head for the mirror for a quick check-up.

But what about all that stuff that doesn't show up in the mirror? What about our hidden resentments, hot-tempered tendencies, or self-centered outlook on life? Proverbs 27:19 says that in the same way that water reflects a face, a person's heart reflects who that person really is. If only there were mirrors for our hearts.

That's where time for personal reflection comes in. Spending time examining our hearts is immeasurably more important than examining our outward appearance. But does the manner in which we spend our time reflect that fact?

If you can hardly remember the last time you had a moment alone to really think about life, it's time to schedule a personal retreat. This kind of retreat is not like an army on the run. It's a time to review where you've been, reflect on how you're feeling right now, and prepare to fight the battles that lie ahead. It is not a strategy session as much as it is a time to quiet your mind long enough to hear what God is whispering to your heart. Whether you have the luxury of a whole weekend or can set aside a day, or just an afternoon, it is time well invested in helping you become who God created you to be.

Though we could all use a vacation, think of a retreat as a working vacation. Take along a journal to write down what you learn, questions you're still wrestling with, and steps you want to put into practice. If your time of reflection doesn't cause you to take action, it really isn't any more useful than the time you spend looking in the mirror each morning. Then don't forget to plan your next retreat. Getting a date and time on your calendar is the best way to ensure it is more than one of those "I'll get around to it someday" ideas.

But why wait until your next personal retreat to reflect on where you are today? Why not take a few moments every morning for a quick heart check? Ask yourself a few simple questions. What areas am I growing in? Where could I use a little help? Is there anyone I need to apologize to? Is there anyone I need to thank? Don't forget to invite God into your time of reflection. He's the only mirror that can help you look deeply enough into your heart to see what's really hidden inside.

CHAPTER 13

*He is invited to do great things
who receives small things greatly.*

CASSIODORUS

It Isn't Easy Being the Invisible Man, but It's Worth It

W hat if you did something heroic, something of epic proportions . . . saved a city from an impending meteorite, rescued a princess from an evil giant, or put your life on the line for someone you'd never met? How would you feel if no one offered a simple word of thanks? Or suppose someone else got all of the credit for your noble deeds? Would not being recognized for the sacrifices you'd made, or the risks you'd taken, leave you bitter? The next time you saw someone in need of help, would you consider turning the other way?

You and I may never be presented with the opportunity to make a "front page news" kind of sacrifice. But every single day is filled with opportunities to take on the job of a servant. The problem is that servanthood has such an unappealing job description: putting someone else's needs before your own, doing exhausting jobs at inconvenient times for nothing in return, all the while risking criticism from those who feel your time would be better spent doing something more important.

The phrase "no guts, no glory" does not hold true for a servant. "Guts, but no glory" would be far more accurate. It's easy to work hard when you know you'll receive recognition. When you'll get that trophy for your mantle, those accolades from your coworkers, that fifteen minutes of fame.

If you're seeking recognition, servanthood is not a great place to find it. In fact, being a servant may require your being invisible all together. It may mean visiting someone in the hospital who will never remember you came, picking up someone else's trash, volunteering to serve meals to people who cannot bring themselves to look you in the eye, or donating money to help a family that will never know your name.

The want-ads crying out for the help of anyone with a servant's heart are posted everywhere. They are found on the park bench, sleeping under a newspaper, or right next door in the overflowing laundry basket of an overwhelmed new mom. You can spot them on the front pages of the newspaper or in the prayer requests shared at a church potluck. But these cries for help often go unnoticed by those who are busily trying to make sure that their own needs are not only met, but exceeded. We cannot be servants if our eyes are not open enough to recognize the opportunities for service all around us.

Need help recognizing those opportunities? Ask God to open your eyes. Then ask for direction from someone who you've seen exhibits a servant's heart. Take any job, at first. Once you begin to see the needs around you, it is more likely that you'll be overwhelmed, not underworked. Just remember that it is not our responsibility to meet the needs of the entire world. Our only responsibility is to meet the needs that God has specifically set aside for us as individuals.

Take into account your natural talents and abilities, your material resources, and the needs that most deeply touch your heart. You don't have to travel across the globe to be a servant. It may take more humility to deal with the needs you see in your own neighborhood.

No need is too small or insignificant for a servant. Opening a door for a mother with four toddlers in tow counts as much as organizing a clothing drive for the homeless shelter. We just can't forget to check our invisibility quotient now and then. If serving others gives our pride a buzz because it makes us feel like the oh-so-generous benefactor, we may need to step back for a while. A true servant is motivated by love, not the need to feel needed.

True servants also know how to accept help when they find themselves in need of it. Having someone give you money, help you move, or watch your kids without asking for anything in return can be a humbling experience. But we are all better servants when we remember what it feels like to be served.

Why not take a moment and ask God to open your eyes to a need you can meet for someone else today? Your prayer just may be the answer to someone else's cry for help.

CHAPTER 14

Pray not for crutches, but for wings!

PHILIP BROOKS

WISE MEN, AND WOMEN, ALWAYS STOP AND ASK FOR DIRECTIONS

When do you pray? With your kids before bedtime? Before a traditional Thanksgiving meal? When the pastor at church asks everyone to bow their heads? At weddings and funerals? When the diagnosis includes the word "cancer"? When you really, really, really want something?

Prayer fits in anytime, anywhere. It doesn't matter whether you close your eyes, bow your head, kneel, whisper, or even utter any words at all. There are no passwords or secret handshakes. However, when you get right down to it, prayer is simply spending time with God. It's having a conversation—with Someone you cannot see.

That's the tricky part. It reminds us that this isn't your typical conversation. After all, we're speaking to the God of the universe. That sounds pretty important, like we ought to throw in some "Thees" and "Thous," and perhaps even a "Your Honor" or two.

That's the true wonder of prayer. The God who created us wants to speak with us. He wants to hear our hopes and dreams and fears. He encourages us to share our wants and needs. He looks forward to us asking Him for direction. He revels in spending time with us. With puny, little us.

One problem with this Big God/little us arrangement is that it can lead us to regard God as a giant E-Bay in the sky. All we do is submit our prayer request. Say we want sun for a party we've scheduled on Saturday morning. We figure if there aren't more people who pray for rain that day, we should get our request. Saturday arrives and we expect delivery. What happens in our heart when it snows?

This is when people begin to doubt whether prayer works or if God is even listening at all. They may try praying harder, longer, or asking others to pray with them. They may even try fasting, to give their prayer request a little extra leverage.

But God is not a vending machine. We don't plug in what we want, pay with our good deeds, and automatically get our request. There's a catch. What we pray for must line up with God's will. Just take a look at the Lord's Prayer if you need some verification.

Prayer is not so much a grocery list of wants as it is a time to get our will aligned with God's. When we decide to ask Him for that yacht we've always wanted, what we may wind up with instead is a better understanding of our pride and greed. It's true that sometimes this feels like asking for a snowmobile for Christmas and ending up with gift certificates for counseling. But God is more concerned with our needs than our wants. He's more concerned with who we are than what we have. And deep down we are too.

Taking time to talk with God is more than just saying "gimme, gimme, gimme." It is time to thank Him for all He's given us already. Praise Him for who He is. Tell Him how much you really love Him. Share your pain, concerns, and confusion. Bask in the knowledge of knowing that He's near. Take time to stop talking and listen. (More about that in the next chapter!)

If taking time every day to talk to God is a new concept for you, you may wonder how to start. The key is to start right now. Just tell God how much you want to get to know Him better. You can do this either out loud or silently. You can even write your prayers down, kind of like talking to God while you journal. You can read the book of Psalms to get a feel for how honestly others have spoken to Him. You can pray with a friend over the phone or in person.

First Thessalonians 5:17 tells us to pray all the time. That doesn't mean we should sit in a corner and never talk to anyone other than God. It just means that God should be an integral part of our day. He should be invited into every decision we make and blessing we celebrate. All we need to do is be open and honest. We don't have to worry about hurting His feelings. God has undoubtedly heard the same doubts and complaints and questions before. All He wants is to help us get to know Him better.

Prayer doesn't always guarantee a change in circumstances. However, it *does* guarantee a change in us. Prayer helps bring our character, and perspective, more in line with the One we're spending time with. Talk about a good influence! Why not take a moment right now just to thank God for the privilege we have of striking up a conversation with Him?

CHAPTER 15

The will of God will never lead you

where the grace of God cannot keep you.

ANONYMOUS

LISTEN FOR THE WHISPER OF HEAVEN

The phone rings. The chances of it being a telemarketer are pretty high at this time of day, but you chance it. Your "hello" is met with a familiar, "What's up?" You relax, grab your cup of coffee, and head for the nearest recliner. It's going to be another marathon call. How do you know? You'd recognize the voice of your best friend anywhere. You know what to expect.

Recognizing the voice of someone you love doesn't take any special talent. It's a skill that is developed naturally over time. The more time you spend together, the quicker you pick it up. But does the same hold true for recognizing the voice of God?

Today, most people who publicly proclaim they hear God's voice are labeled fanatics, egomaniacs, or, at the least, mentally unstable. The question is, does God really speak to us today? And if so, what does He sound like? We've all heard about those impressive encounters in the Bible's Old Testament: God speaking out of a burning bush, a pillar of fire, or thunder on a mountaintop. But God didn't always rely on flashy special effects as the means to carry His message.

In the book of 1 Kings, a man named Elijah desperately wanted to hear God's voice. Elijah was depressed. Really depressed. He'd given the people of Israel the message God had told him to deliver. But it seemed that no one wanted to hear what Elijah had to say. Elijah felt alone and defeated. He even feared for his life.

So Elijah called out to God. He knew it was time for a serious chat. A powerful windstorm erupted around him. The winds were so strong that it sent rocks tumbling down the side of the mountain where Elijah stood. But Elijah knew that God was not in the wind. Once the wind calmed down, an earthquake shook the ground. But Elijah could tell that God was not in the earthquake. Next came a raging fire. But once again, Elijah did not hear God's voice in the flames. After the fire died down, it seemed as though everything was still. Except, that is, for the sound of a gentle whisper. When Elijah heard the whisper, He recognized the voice of God.

To understand someone who is speaking to you in a whisper, you need to move away from other distractions. You need to draw near to the one speaking. You cannot be talking at the same time. You need to give that person your full attention, or you'll miss what's being said. Maybe that's why God seems to choose a whisper over a burning bush these days. A whisper makes us stop and really listen.

Have you heard God's whisper in your life? Perhaps you've heard it through what's written in the Bible. Maybe you detected it in the honest words of someone close to you. Or it could have been through circumstances, especially your pain, where God's whisper caught your ear. Or was it through His quiet, gentle promptings in your heart?

If you're having trouble hearing God's voice, perhaps it's because you just don't recognize it yet. To hear God speak, we need to draw close to Him, spend time with Him, listen long enough to pick up even a faint whisper.

Being able to pick out God's soft voice above the shouts of the rest of life takes practice. Life may be shouting, "You've blown it!" "Give up!" "Forget about integrity—just do whatever it takes to earn more money!" Life's taunts often seem brutal and relentless.

In contrast, the words God whispers are grounded in love and truth: "You matter." "I forgive you." "Your pain hasn't been wasted." "I will always love you." God's words help us head the right direction in life. They let us know what action we should take. They correct us when we're wrong. They encourage us when we're down. They tell us the truth about who we really are.

When God whispers, are you close enough to hear what He has to say?

CHAPTER 16

*Earth has no sorrow
that Heaven cannot heal.*

THOMAS MOORE

THE BLUES IS MORE THAN A TUNE ON THE RADIO

When was your last mountaintop experience? You know the kind I mean. You find yourself filled with incredible joy, overwhelmed by seemingly impossible beauty, so grateful just to be alive that you can scarcely keep your feet from dancing. Sometimes it comes upon you in a flash, brought on by the sight of a blazing sunset or the face of a long lost friend. Or perhaps it's something that builds to a crescendo as you near the end of what seems like a perfect day.

I remember one such moment that brought me even higher than a mountaintop. It took place in the window seat of a plane. We were flying over water, lots of water, which is usually a fairly boring endeavor. But just the right combination of clouds, sunshine, crystal clear waters, shallow island inlets, and even the sun-resistant coating of the plane window, worked together to create a moving work of art. Blues, purples, iridescent greens, and golds all combined beneath me like a Monet-esque view of the world. The kaleidoscope of colors continued to swirl: one minute opaque, then translucent.

I hit my husband in the ribs. "Honey, look!" He glanced up from his book. "What?" he replied. "The colors!" I said with delight. "Uh-huh," he murmured as he returned to his book. Apparently, one person's mountaintop can obviously be another's interruption.

I went back to my own reverie, spending almost an hour delighting in the magic that was going on beneath me. What made that time even more precious was the fact that I had spent the last several weeks wallowing in depression. There was nothing horribly wrong in my life. But my emotions just couldn't seem to get in touch with that fact. But somehow beauty and wonder had broken through the darkness that had seemed to surround me. I could hardly find the words to thank God for the unexpected gift.

Depression can be a normal reaction to the tragedies of life or a persistent sense of doom and gloom that seems to come out of nowhere. Either way, it is not something to be ignored. Everyone has a case of the blues now and then. But if they last for more than a few weeks, it's time to ask for help. Letting depression go unchecked can actually change your brain chemistry, making it harder to get rid of that sense of despondency.

Your doctor, or a mental health professional, can help you rule out possible causes such as hormonal changes, a deficient thyroid, repressed anger, or exhaustion.

But how do you handle those occasional down times that come your way? What do you do when nothing's really wrong, but you just don't feel quite right? Start by talking about it. Though calling a good friend is a great thing to do, it's not the only way to talk about how you feel. You can also write your feelings in a journal or have a chat with your Heavenly Father.

Along with talking, it also helps to listen to what people who know just how you feel have to say. People like that are as close as the book of Psalms. These are people who have been so down that they begged God to let them die. They've been so angry that they asked God to get rid of their enemies in rather creatively vindictive ways. They are also people who felt free enough with God to voice their doubts and their questions to Him when they felt that life was unfair. But throughout the Psalms, one thing remains true. The psalmists didn't remain in the depths of their depression. After expressing their feelings to God, they wound up praising Him. They ended up back on top of that mountain.

But mountaintop experiences don't last forever. Life is filled with highs and lows. If you've ever climbed a mountain, you know that after you've reached the summit and taken a look around, eventually it's time to go back down. The top is barren and exposed to the elements. It's not a particularly pretty place. All of the dynamic growth that happens on a mountain happens below tree line. It's exhilarating standing on that mountaintop for a while, but the real living takes place on the slopes; and even, on occasion, in the valleys below.

Just don't spend so much time in the valley that you start singing the blues.

CHAPTER 17

The shy one will not learn;

the impatient man should not teach.

Ask and learn.

HILLEL THE ELDER

You Can't Teach an Old Broad New Tricks . . . or Can You?

In the 1920s, Helen was a promising Rhodes scholar attending Oxford University in England. With a new graduate's degree and her first published book, Helen arrived back in the United States with the hope of a promising career in writing. Instead, she faced the Great Depression. But that did not put an end to her dreams. It merely put them on hold.

In 1984, Helen Hoover Santmyer's . . . *And the Ladies of the Club* was the best-selling book of the year. At that time, Santmyer was a spry eighty-eight years old. Perhaps writing wasn't a new trick for Santmyer, but it certainly wasn't one most people would have expected her to still put to good use as she approached her nineties.

Of course, women don't have a monopoly on continuing to learn and grow as they age. When a literacy volunteer knocked on George Dawson's door in south Dallas and told him that adult education courses were being held a few blocks away, he responded enthusiastically, "Wait! I'll get my coat!" Dawson not only learned to read at ninety-eight years of age, but published his memoirs four years later.

Learning is something that doesn't stop after high school or college, unless you let it. Every day is a classroom filled with endless curriculum. What you choose to learn is up to you. Are there any skills you have always wanted to acquire, such as playing a musical instrument or speaking a foreign language? Recent research has shown that learning skills such as these is not only a personally satisfying pursuit, but that continuing this type of complex learning as we age can actually help guard against the onset of Alzheimer's. So pick up a book. Sign up for a class. Hire a tutor. Raise your IQ. Practice skills you've already acquired that are beginning to get a bit rusty. Don't be afraid to try something new. You may uncover a passion, or talent, you never knew you had.

But you and I have the capacity to learn much more than skills. We can also learn how to become better people. For instance, we can become more compassionate, forgiving, generous, or patient. As we put into practice what we learn from our own life experience and the experiences of others, we continue to mature. Maturity has little to do with chronological age.

Some of us grow older without growing wiser. That means we keep aging but stop learning and prudently using what we're learning along the way.

We've talked about how our pursuit of knowledge shouldn't end. But did you know that knowledge has a clear-cut beginning? Proverbs 1:7 says that knowledge begins with the fear of God. This kind of fear has more to do with awe than with terror. It comes from knowing who God is. It comes from getting a glimpse of God's power, love, and holiness. It comes from recognizing that God is the only One we should ever bow down to.

This knowledge comes from several sources. The Bible gives us the best picture of who God is and how we can get to know

Him better. Other excellent resources are personal prayer, getting involved in a local church, and asking questions of those who are further along on their journey of faith than we are. Best of all, God has promised that His Spirit will give us a better knowledge of Him. All we need to do is ask.

Being wise and being knowledgeable are two different things. But when knowledge begins with an understanding of God's character, our wisdom will continue to grow by merely acting on what we know.

If you didn't learn everything you needed to know in kindergarten, it isn't too late. Learn something new today. Then share what you've learned with someone else. The desire to learn and grow is often contagious.

CHAPTER 18

The man who removes a mountain

begins by carrying away small stones.

CHINESE PROVERB

By Perseverance the Snail Reached the Ark

The job was not a particularly difficult one. Put one syllabus on the seat of each chair in the class. My son was doing a great job with the tedious task—until we reached the auditorium. When Ryan saw hundreds of chairs, instead of the usual forty to fifty, he panicked. To say he ran screaming from the room is not much of an exaggeration.

It was time for a little chat. After all, the job was exactly the same one Ryan had done earlier that morning. Put one syllabus on the seat of each chair. Ryan was overwhelmed by the size of the job, not the job itself. His success was merely a matter of focus and perseverance.

Perseverance is the ability to keep moving, even when you can only take small steps. It's concentrating on connecting piece A to piece B and forgetting about pieces X, Y, and ZZZ. It's choosing to focus on the details: "How do you eat an elephant?" One bite at a time, my friend, one bite at a time.

But perseverance is not without its potholes. It's easy to get tired, discouraged, or sidetracked along the way. Once any of these problems take hold, it's easy to lose hope. And once hope is lost, it takes a fresh start to get moving again.

Williamette Rudolph was a woman who needed a fresh start, even though she was only thirteen years of age. After contracting polio as a young child, Willie wore leg braces through most of her childhood. But at the age of thirteen, it was time for the braces to be removed. It was a turning point in Willie's life. She knew her legs were weaker than the other kids'. It would have been easy for Willie to sit back while other kids her age played basketball and skipped rope. Instead, she began running to strengthen her legs. Willie not only caught up with the other kids, but surpassed them. At the age of twenty, Willie became the fastest woman on earth. She won three gold medals in track at the 1960 Olympics.

What helped Willie persevere was her perspective. She saw possibility where others saw disability. She focused on how far she had come, instead of how far she had to go. Is there any area of your life where you could use a fresh perspective? Is there any area where you've given up? Take a lesson from my son. Tackle it one chair at a time.

God's on your side. He knows how difficult it is to persevere. Eighty years of life may be a gift, but it's too much to handle all at one time. That's why God broke down our lives into days. He designed our bodies to need breaks for food and rest. He created us to live in community so there would be others to encourage us along the way. And when God had a big project ahead of Him, creating the world, He didn't try to do it all at once. He did it one chair at a time. He created the heavens and the earth, then light, and plants, and animals, and us. He persevered through aardvarks and zinnias until He knew He was finished. He looked over everything He'd made and commented, "Job well done." Then He took a day off. What better example could there be for us to follow?

CHAPTER 19

If you tell the truth,

you don't have to remember anything.

MARK TWAIN

The Best Policy Is Still Honesty

The party at the table next to us was in a quandary. My girlfriend and I didn't mean to eavesdrop. But this extremely colorful and boisterous group of folks was tough to ignore in an intimate restaurant setting. The waitress had forgotten to charge them for one of the meals they'd ordered. The animated discussion that followed went something like this . . .

"Oh, man, this can't be right!" "Well, maybe it's some kind of special or something." "We gotta go!" "Why don't we just leave a bigger tip?" "But what if they take the difference out of her paycheck?" "Hey, if we don't make this right, think of the bad karma it'll bring!"

They called the waitress over to look at the bill.

Why is honesty the best policy? Maybe what some people regard as bad karma is simply the natural consequences of doing something that destroys instead of builds, something that God repeatedly speaks out against. The consequences of dishonesty include guilt, the fear of being caught, and a loss of integrity in the eyes of others.

The first step away from honesty toward deception begins with lying to yourself. "It's not like it's going to hurt anyone," you rationalize. "No one will ever find out," you try and convince yourself. "It's just a little white lie," you minimize. A white lie is still a lie.

Granted, exaggerating a story to get a bigger laugh seems rather insignificant when compared to cheating on your taxes or lying on a resumé. However, dishonesty of any kind ends up being a trap. One lie has to be covered with another. And somehow the next lie seems just a little easier.

But dishonesty covers up a deeper problem. It usually stems from pride, fear, or greed, the real areas of our character we need to work on. Like the time my SUV munched the bumper of a parked car. (Notice I placed the blame on the SUV. How honest is that?) I wanted to drive away. "No one saw me," I tried to convince myself. "It's only a little dent," I minimized. "I don't have the money to pay for this," I rationalized.

I didn't want to take responsibility for what I'd done. I wanted someone else to pay my debt. But I wrote the driver a note, leaving my phone number. When he called, do you know what he said? "My car has been hit three times in the last year, and you are the first person who didn't just drive away. Thanks."

Proverbs 24:26 says that an honest answer is like a warm embrace. Honesty fosters unity and community, instead of division. It allows relationships to go beyond superficiality to unconditional love. An added personal benefit is that it gives us freedom. We no longer have to look over our shoulders, wondering if a police officer is going to ultimately track us down for hitting a car in a parking lot. We don't have to remember what lies we've told in fear of contradicting them. We are free to be who we truly are and what God has created us to be. Honest.

CHAPTER 20

One day in perfect health is much.

ARABIAN PROVERB

BUICKS DON'T RUN ON CHOCOLATE

Automobiles are meant to run on the proper fuel, whether it's leaded, unleaded, or diesel. Imagine what would happen if you filled your gas tank with chocolate syrup. Good stuff, but not from your engine's point of view.

Our bodies need proper maintenance just like our automobiles. They need the right fuel. They need regular check-ups. They need a little extra attention so they don't overheat in the summer sun. They run best when those who use them do what the owner's manual recommends. Which are you more meticulous about, the care of your automobile or your body?

Consider your sleep patterns. Do you drive your body until it falls apart or do you actually pull into the garage now and then? Although people differ as to the hours of sleep they require, most people need between seven and nine hours a night. That doesn't include the time it takes you to fall asleep or the time you spend in the morning hitting the snooze button. How many uninterrupted hours do you usually receive? Although you can "make up" a few hours one night if you deprive yourself the day before, sleeping in until noon every Saturday won't make up for night after night of sleep deprivation.

Everyone can relate to that groggy feeling when we're running on too little sleep. But it's not just our brains that aren't working efficiently. It's our bodies themselves. Sleep deprivation can make us more susceptible to illness. It can even make us gain weight. How's that for depressing?

Sleep is physical fuel, just like the food we eat. It's been said that if we are what we eat, many of us would be fast, cheap, and easy. What does your diet say about you? Living in a country where food is overly abundant is a mixed blessing for millions of Americans. For many of us, food is not just fuel. It's a reward, a pastime, a comforting friend. That's why dieting doesn't always work. If we don't change whatever we're trying to fill in our lives with food—other than just hunger—we're not solving a problem. We're trying to sidestep it.

And how about those regular check-ups? Some of us figure that what we don't know can't hurt us. At least, we act as though that's true. But long-term survival rates of potentially life-threatening diseases that are detected early should be enough to debunk that fallacy.

So how does any of this relate to maturing as an individual? Just turn to the owner's manual, better known as the Bible. First Corinthians 6:19 asks us if we know that our bodies are God's temple. How would you answer that question? Think of your physical body for a moment. Not just its appearance, but what you put into it and how well-tuned you keep it. Does it remind you more of a temple or a truck stop?

The next verse in 1 Corinthians reminds us that we show honor to God by how we treat His creation, our physical bodies. If we desire a character that brings honor to God, why wouldn't we want our bodies to do the same?

The physical form of every individual has its own quirks and weaknesses, and sometimes even handicaps and long-term illnesses. We each have a choice as to how we are going to respond to what we've been given. Will we accept the one-of-a-kind gift of our physical body? Will we use it to the best of its potential ability? Will we care for it like the fragile instrument that it is? Or will we take it for granted, wearing it out before its time? The decision is up to each of us.

CHAPTER 21

———— ⌒ ————

May you live all the days of your life.

———————————

JONATHAN SWIFT

SOMETIMES PASSION'S FIRE COULD USE A LITTLE LIGHTER FLUID

My home rocks. Literally. No, it wasn't built on an earthquake fault. The basement has just been designated "rehearsal central" for my church's two live bands. Believe me, this is not Aunt Martha on the Wurlitzer. We are talking electric guitar, bass, keyboard, and drums, not to mention the occasional brass section. It's a good thing our neighbors are music lovers.

Both bands are composed of gifted individuals with a real love of music. But there is a difference between the adult band and the high school band. The high school band originally began rehearsing for an hour every Thursday. That grew to an hour and a half, two hours, and then three. They'd probably stay longer if the adult band didn't show up for a rehearsal of their own.

Every Thursday afternoon, the floorboards of my kitchen shake. Rising up from the basement through the heating vents is the sound of singing, laughter, and jam sessions that go on longer than it takes to prepare dinner. I usually descend only to throw a pizza or two to the hungry masses, but what I see while I'm there is kids having fun.

Now the members of the adult band are certainly not prudes. They know how to rock and have a good time as well. But most of them have rushed here after a long day at work and still have things to attend to once they get home. Once the time for rehearsal to end has arrived, they are "outta here."

It's not that the adult band isn't passionate about what they're doing. They are. But they are also tired. After you've been passionate about something for a while, it's easy for that passion to lose some of its fire. It begins to feel comfortable, predictable, even mundane. Somewhere along the way, you've lost that first love.

Has it happened to you? Perhaps it's a profession that you dreamed of pursuing since you were a kid. Now, just getting up and going to work feels like a punishment instead of a privilege. Or maybe it's your marriage. Sure, you still like each other. But after fifteen years, it seems more like a business relationship than a romance. Or perhaps it's your relationship with God. Studying the Bible seems more like homework than chatting with the God of the universe.

It's time to recapture your first love. What made you first fall in love with your spouse, pursue your profession, believe in God? How did you feel? Why? Most things we are truly passionate about are more than a passing fancy. There is something in us that resonates with that particular person or thing. But part of passion involves mystery. Once we know everything about something, the adventure seems to have hit a dead end. But the real secret is that there's always more to learn. There are new adventures ahead. Perhaps we just need to shake up the status quo.

For instance, every marriage develops certain patterns: who pays the bills, who cleans the toilets, what signals the start of a romantic interlude. Don't let habit lull you into taking your spouse for granted or convince you that "the thrill is gone." Turn off the TV, turn up the stereo, and dance together. Send flowers. Try something new at the dinner table or in the bedroom. Kiss your spouse, just because. Try and discover one new thing about your spouse every day.

Or why not learn one new thing about God every day? Pray out loud instead of silently. Talk with someone about why he or she believes in God. Write your own psalm. Read the autobiography of someone whose faith you admire. Take a walk with God and just chat about all the great things He's made. Write Him a thank you note. Or paint Him a picture.

As for your job? Take a class to learn new skills. Talk to your boss about revamping your job description. If you've been dreaming of a job change, stop dreaming and go for it. (See, "Life's Too Short to Do What You Hate!") Don't just work harder; work smarter. Figure out where you really shine. Then go ahead and shine.

Every so often, I see my church's adult band really shine during rehearsal. It usually happens when they get off track. It's when strains of "Wipeout" or "Mission Impossible" creep into the mix. When they forget they are working and begin having fun. That's when the pilot light of passion's fire gets relit. That taste of the unexpected stirs the embers of their passion enough to get them hyped about Sunday morning. It keeps them *and* their performance fresh. What can you do to relight the flame of passion in your life?

CHAPTER 22

God's gifts put man's best dreams to shame.

ELIZABETH BARRETT BROWNING

Don't Just Count Your Blessings— Say Thank You

———— ⌒◦⌒ ————

From the outside, BJ's looks as though it's on the verge of being condemned. The weathered, wooden sign sporting a smiling ice cream cone could use a new coat of paint. The photographs in the smudged windows showing burgers, pork sandwiches, and onion rings have faded to an unappetizing swamp green. There is no inside seating. But there are two picnic tables nearby, usually sporting a few scattered splotches of ketchup and ice cream. From the oversized wooden benches, there is an exhaust-filled view of the busy street corner and the gas station next door.

Unfortunately, since BJ's is located in Colorado, it's only open the five months out of the year when the snow doesn't fly. And that is a real shame. BJ's has some of the best food around, especially when it comes to ice cream. Their specialty is a Boston Shake. That's a milkshake with a sundae built on top of it.

Armed with both a spoon and a straw, there's only a 50/50 chance that you can finish it without spilling yet more ice cream onto the grimy picnic tables. And the onion rings, well . . . we'll just stop there. Health food, it's not. But my family usually goes with our standard favorite, a BJ's shake. Whether it's blackberry, marshmallow, or my personal favorite, banana hot fudge, these milkshakes inspire my family to drive twenty minutes out of our way to sit on uncomfortable wooden benches, slurp, and smile.

One summer day we were doing just that. My teenage daughter Katrina had just taken a big sip of her customary butterscotch shake. She gave a deep sigh and then asked, "Why can't the last sip of a milkshake taste just as good as the first?"

Good question. We all know that "too much of a good thing" dulls our senses. But it's amazing how little it takes before we begin taking things for granted, forgetting that first taste of pleasure that made us enjoy, and appreciate, something in the first place.

It can be as small a pleasure as enjoying a great milkshake or as grand an experience as moving into your dream home. The novelty seems to wear off before the milkshake is finished or the house needs to be repainted. It can even happen in relationships. Once the honeymoon is over, that seven-year itch isn't all that far down the road.

So, how do we change? Is there any way to make that milkshake taste "good to the last drop"? We can begin by slowing down. What holds true when enjoying a butterscotch shake follows through into the rest of life. Sip, don't gulp. Savor one thing at a time. Make an effort to experience it fully. If you're on vacation, don't cram seven countries into seven days. If you're spending time with a friend, don't be mentally reviewing your *To Do* list. Listen, linger, saunter, relish, stop and smell the roses. Then remember to say "thanks."

Cultivating an attitude of gratitude begins with recognizing how many ways we've been blessed each day. That includes ordinary days, Mondays, and even the day after vacation is over, when you're faced with a pile of dirty laundry. One way to increase your awareness of how richly you've been blessed is to take a few minutes each morning to write down your blessings in a journal: "good night's sleep, promotion at work, enough groceries, time with Mom . . ." Your list can contain anything, big or small, that has had a positive effect on your life.

Then let that list be a springboard for thanks. If you're thankful that your next door neighbor mowed your lawn while you were out of town, take a moment to write a note, give him a call, or at least stop by and say how much you appreciate not just what he did, but who he is. And don't forget to take a moment for a word of thanks to the One who blesses us each and every day in more ways than we could ever keep track of in a journal. The more we appreciate what God has done in our lives, the more our eyes will be opened to recognize blessings we could have easily overlooked.

That's why it makes sense to pray before we eat. It's not just a tradition. Giving thanks to God for what's on our plates reminds us that the food we often take for granted isn't guaranteed. It's really a blessing straight from God's hand. A big one. And recognizing that fact is not only the right thing to do, it slows us down enough to enjoy the meal before us. That helps even a milkshake taste better, right down to the last drop.

CHAPTER 23

*The Bible is a letter from God
with our personal address on it.*

SØREN KIERKEGAARD

SOME BESTSELLERS ARE ACTUALLY WORTH READING

"Forgive and forget." "Cleanliness is next to godliness." "Money is the root of all evil." "God helps those who help themselves." "Honesty is the best policy." "Idle hands are the devil's workshop." "Practice what you preach." "Time heals all wounds." "Waste not, want not."

How many of these proverbs are found in the Bible? Actually, none. But it's amazing what some people take as the gospel truth. Take the one about money being the root of all evil. This proverb differs from what is written in the Bible by one little word: "love." First Timothy 6:10 tells us that the *love* of money is at the root of all kinds of evil. One little word makes one big difference.

What do you really know about the Bible? Is what you know based on hearsay or personal experience? Learning about the Bible through what is preached at church, written in inspirational books, or voiced through the opinions of others is a good place to start. But you can't really *know* the Bible until you've actually spent time reading it.

Granted, getting acquainted can be rather daunting. The first time you pick it up, it looks a bit like *War and Peace.* Lengthy. Tiny print. No pictures. And if you tackle it like any other book, beginning with page one, you'll soon wind up plowing through a bunch of genealogies filled with multi-syllabic, unpronounceable names. In other words, you'll probably put it down and wonder if this book has any relevance at all to helping you become the person God created you to be.

But wait. The Bible isn't your typical bestseller, even though more copies of it are sold than any other book in the world. It was written by 39 different authors over the course of 3000 years. It was completed about 2000 years ago and contains 66 different books. In other words, there's a whole lot of stuff in there. And Cliff's Notes are really not an option.

The Bible isn't a novel to be read in one sitting. It's something to be studied, and yes, even enjoyed. But it is best served in small bites, chewed slowly over time. Written in several different genres, the Bible contains history, poetry, prophecy, and even letters. Through it all, one thing rings true: God is involved in what happens on this earth. He cares about every individual, from all of those folks with the unpronounceable names right down to you and me. That's why its message is just as relevant to our lives today as it was to Methuselah and Zerubbabel.

Filled with stories of good guys and bad guys, the Bible displays people who succeeded as well as people who failed, individuals who followed God and those who turned the other way. It brings together a crowd of imperfect people . . . people you and I can relate to . . . people with whom God wasn't finished yet. So why not take the time to learn from their mistakes and victories?

One of the best places to start reading is the Gospels—Matthew, Mark, Luke, and John. Then, read a few shorter Epistles, or letters, that follow them. Read one Psalm and one chapter of Proverbs a day. These are also a good way to get practical advice on right living from one part of the Bible, while at the same time in the other part, you will empathize with those who questioned God when life didn't make sense. After you feel more at home with the Bible, you may even find yourself heading back toward those genealogies—and liking it.

When you come upon something you don't understand, don't be afraid to ask for help. You can get clarity on some of the more obscure passages from other reference materials, through what you learn at church, or by asking those who've had more experience reading the Bible than you have. Just don't forget to first ask the Author for insight. Praying before you begin reading, and then over anything that's unclear, will help you better understand and apply what you learn.

Just remember that this bestseller isn't a textbook. Its sole purpose is not to be analyzed and memorized, even though both of those things can play a part in understanding what's written. It's a love letter from the One who made you. Just like reading a letter from someone helps you to better know his or her heart, the Bible helps us understand God's character and how He longs to restore ours.

CHAPTER 24

*The most valuable of all talents
is that of never using two words
when one will do.*

THOMAS JEFFERSON

A Closed Mouth Gathers No Foot

"Sticks and stones may break my bones, but names will never hurt me!" Yeah, right. When you're in elementary school, the only defense you have against being made fun of is to either start a fight (frowned on by both parents and the school's administration) or pretend that whatever was said about you doesn't matter. As adults, it is time that we master a few more options.

The truth is, words do matter. A lot. The book of Proverbs is filled with lessons about the power of the spoken word. Take Proverbs 12:18, for example. It equates reckless words to a piercing sword. At the same time, it reminds us that wise words bring healing. In Proverbs 25:11, the perfect word spoken at the perfect time is likened to a beautiful piece of jewelry, apples of gold in a setting of silver.

Throughout the Bible, words are described in only two ways. They either hurt or heal. They are a tree of life or a raging fire. They are a weapon or a gift. They are either foolish or wise—never neutral.

Our days are filled with words. We remind the kids not to forget their homework, say "I love you" to our spouse, tell the telemarketer we're not interested, ask the clerk where we can find the tofu, order lunch, reprimand the dog, console a friend, and greet a new coworker. Almost every interaction we have with another person involves words. What we say, and the tone of voice with which we say it, fashions our words into a weapon or a gift.

Often we don't think much about it. We just talk. But if every word we say has so much power, not thinking before we speak is almost like playing with matches. A careless word can damage a relationship or break someone's heart. Unfortunately, we may be so busy babbling that we're not even aware of it.

That's why we need to stop, look, and listen. The first step to getting our tongues under control is to STOP long enough to pay attention to what's coming out of our mouths. Picture a tape recorder hanging around your neck. At the end of the day, if you listened to the tape, how much of what you said would really be helpful, useful, or even necessary?

We humans like to hear the sound of our own voices. We hate for our opinions to go unheard or our grievances to go unnoticed. So we jump into conversations, interrupt others, and battle to have the last word. Can we actually stop long enough to keep our mouths shut? That isn't as easy as it sounds. There's something about putting our two cents in that makes us feel important and included. That leads us right into step number two. We need to LOOK at why we're opening our mouths in the first place.

Are we imparting important information? Or do we just think we are because we feel our opinion is so much more valuable than the opinions of those around us? Do we want to impress others or have them laugh at our jokes? Are we trying to make ourselves appear to be someone we're not? Do we just want to fit in? Are we attempting to fill in dead air, because silence makes us uncomfortable?

Looking at the "whys" behind our words will help us speak wiser words. But before we can really impart a verbal gift to others, we need to actually LISTEN to what they have to say. If we are thinking about what we want to say, looking for that brief pause when someone takes a breath so we can jump in with our incredible insight, we'll miss what others are really saying to us.

The secret of being a good conversationalist is not eloquence; it's patience. It's giving someone else your full attention. Trying to read their body language, as well as their words. Trying to empathize, then wisely analyze. Sometimes that may mean having to tell someone, "Let me think about what you said for a while" before you respond. When the time, your motives, and your words are right, then you can pass on an apple of gold in a setting of silver. Those are words that will make a positive difference—words worth remembering.

CHAPTER 25

*The art of living is more
like wrestling than dancing.*

MARCUS AURELIUS

THE SQUEAKY WHEEL MAY BE TRYING TO TELL YOU SOMETHING

"Your car is on fire!" Not the words you want to hear from a passing motorist on a leisurely Sunday afternoon drive. My girlfriend and I were thankful that at least someone let us know. We'd been so deep in conversation that we probably wouldn't have noticed a problem until we couldn't see each other through the smoke.

After pulling over onto the shoulder of the highway, we opened the hood of the car. Isn't that what you're supposed to do when something is wrong? Of course all I know about cars is how to fill them with gas, check the oil, add windshield washer fluid, and drive them to the mechanic. My girlfriend had a bit more automotive savvy, but flames coming from the engine was a bit out of either of our areas of expertise.

We grabbed out purses and began walking to a nearby truck stop. If the car blew, at least we wouldn't go with it. Besides, it looked like the flames were beginning to die down. We'd call Janelle's husband to come and rescue us and then sit down and finish our conversation. Why waste a beautiful Sunday afternoon?

One thing we didn't do was try to drive the car any farther. We may not be automotively inclined, but both Janelle and I know that when something breaks, ignoring it and trying to go on as though nothing has happened will just make things worse. That bit of wisdom holds true for much more than cars. Take your body, for instance. Suppose an excruciating pain in your chest awakens you from a sound sleep. Do you just hope it will go away or do you call the paramedics? Your life may depend on the course of action you choose.

Pain is usually a signal that something's wrong. It's like the buzzer on an alarm clock, letting you know it's time to do something. But physical pain, or flames from under your car's hood, aren't the only signals we receive in life. When your heart's broken, you receive signals as well. Those signals may be in the form of physical pain. But they may also sound the alarm through depression, anger, fear, overspending, overeating, excessive drinking—the list goes on and on.

Even our relationships with others have signals that let us know when something's wrong. A friend may stop calling. Your spouse may start spending more time at the office than usual. A child may begin locking the door of his or her room. A superior may not include you in an important meeting.

Warning signs are all around us. What we do with them is up to us. We can choose to ignore them and hope they go away. But like driving on a flat tire instead of bothering to stop and change it, we may end up facing a bigger problem down the road. If you get the feeling that something's wrong, face it. Don't blow it out of proportion; just try and figure out what's wrong. And if, like Janelle and I, you don't have a clue, ask for the help of someone who might.

At the top of your 911 list should be God. He can help you determine what is a real problem and what is a false alarm. He won't change a flat for you, but He can give you insight on what to do next. He can also help you become more sensitive to hearing that alarm go off in the first place.

So the next time your brakes start to squeal, your best friend doesn't answer your calls, or you find yourself doing a face plant in a super-sized hot fudge sundae, don't just continue on as though nothing has happened. Figure out what the problem is. Then deal with it. The longer you ignore the squeak, the more accustomed you become to the sound. Eventually, you may even forget it's there. But that doesn't mean the problem has vanished. It only means a louder alarm is going to have to go off before you do something about it. Why wait for flames under your hood? Take care of it now.

CHAPTER 26

God divided man into men,
that they might help each other.

S E N E C A

THAT "LOVE THY NEIGHBOR" THING STILL WORKS

———⌒◠———

Ever since I was a kid, the arrival of the mail has always felt a bit like Christmas. You never know what will be waiting inside your mailbox: a heartfelt thank you note, a newsy letter from a long lost friend, a post card from a traveling relative, a rebate check, a sample of toothpaste, a belated birthday gift—not to mention lots of bills and junk mail. But it's always fun; a bit like searching for hidden treasure.

One day I received a hand-addressed envelope. Thinking it was probably a special note from someone who knew me well, I put aside the advertisements for carpet cleaning and grocery store coupons and excitedly tore open the envelope. Out dropped a newspaper advertisement that read "American Doctors Reveal How a New Discovery from Asia Helps Overcome the Chemical

Imbalance That Keeps People Fat!" Written in ink at the top of the article were the words, "Vicki, try it! It works!"

So I grabbed a couple of chocolate chip cookies and a can of soda and sat down to contemplate this "personal message." Here was someone reaching out to me. Someone deeply concerned about my dress size. Someone who knew it had to be more than my fast food diet that was holding me back from a potential modeling career.

So did I immediately send away for a lifetime supply of this amazing discovery—for which, of course, there was a convenient coupon on the bottom of the page? No way! There was no signature on the handwritten message or even a return address on the envelope. I had no idea who was sharing this generous advice with me. Was someone truly concerned with my weight and health? Or was someone just trying to push a product to make a healthy commission of their own?

Now if my spouse, a neighbor, or a group of close friends had sat me down and brought this article to my attention, expressing their deep concern for my well-being, that would have been a different story. I would have listened and asked questions—perhaps even given the product a try. Why? Because I trust that those people would be reaching out to me because they care, not because they wanted to make a profit.

Who do you reach out to in this world—and why? Most of us have heard of the phrase "love thy neighbor as thyself." But who are our neighbors, and how do we really care for them as much as we do for ourselves? People have been asking that question for centuries. But not everyone really wants to know the answer. That's because loving our neighbor is often inconvenient, time-consuming, and sometimes even downright unpleasant. But it's the only way to build a neighborhood worth living in.

Our neighbors are more than the folks who live on our street. They are anyone we come into contact with during our lives. Every interaction we have with another person is a chance to put love into action, to treat others as we would like to be treated, and to make that golden rule more than just a golden suggestion. It's hard enough to love ourselves in spite of all the areas God is still working on in our lives. Loving others who don't fit our idea of what a neighborly person is like can be a downright struggle.

We've all seen the sign on the back of city service vehicles that reads, "Caution! May stop, back up, and turn around at any time." People are like that—unpredictable. But that's part of what being an individual is all about. Reaching out in love to those unpredictable people can be a challenge. But like most true challenges, the reward that lies ahead is worth the work it takes to get there. If we are reaching out in loving concern for others, really putting ourselves in their place, they'll know it. If, instead, we are really using people, reaching out to them solely to fill our own personal needs, they'll know that as well.

We all long for true community, a sense of belonging, and the comfort of knowing those around us will help us up when we fall. Our only chance of living in that kind of community comes from helping build it, one interaction at a time.

CHAPTER 27

I want it said of me by those who knew me best

that I always plucked a thistle

and planted a flower where I thought

a flower should grow.

ABRAHAM LINCOLN

DON'T MAKE NEVER NEVER LAND YOUR PERMANENT ADDRESS

R emember Peter Pan? He never wanted to grow up. He just wanted to play with his buddies, go to bed whenever he felt like it, and wear the same old thing everyday, dirty or not. He didn't want a job and a home and a family. He wanted life to be fun. And Peter believed that meant he had to call the shots. Period.

But Peter Pan and the Lost Boys were lost in more ways than one. They may have lost their families, but they had also lost their sense of direction. They didn't want to grow up because growing up meant moving forward. And to move forward you not only have to make a decision, but you have to make a commitment to follow through on that decision. What Peter Pan and his friends were afraid of wasn't maturing. It was responsibility.

We can all empathize. Childhood carries with it a certain sense of freedom. Kids don't have to worry about putting food on the table or paying the mortgage. Other people do their laundry and play chauffeur. Kids may have to work at getting their homework in on time, but it isn't a matter of life and death. It's simply a matter of a lower grade. But childhood freedom from responsibility means less freedom in other areas. Grown-ups decide where you'll live, what you'll have for dinner, and how large your allowance will be. As the saying goes, "With privilege comes responsibility." But the reverse also holds true. With responsibility comes privilege.

Have you accepted the fact that as adults we no longer live in Never Never Land? The privileges that come along with adult-hood have a price tag. Their price is responsibility.

Responsibility is more than changing the oil in your car every 3,000 miles or mowing your lawn every Saturday. Responsibility means keeping your promises, even the unspoken ones. When you have a debt, you pay it on time. In return for your paycheck, you give your employer a full day's worth of your best work. When you get married, you don't continue to flirt with the opposite sex. When you say you'll do something, you do it. And if for some reason you fail to fulfill a promise, you take full responsibility. You apologize, make amends, and then begin again.

Are you as good as your word? God is. He's kept every promise He's ever made. God promised the Israelites they'd no longer be slaves. So what did they call the land God led them to? The Promised Land. They knew God well enough not to call it Never Never Land. God delivered on what He had promised.

The same thing could not be said of the Israelites. They repeatedly promised to love God and follow the rules He had set up for their benefit. But they didn't follow through. God had also made promises as to what would happen to the people if they didn't follow Him. Then when He kept His promises, the people got bent out of shape. They wanted to follow Peter Pan and the Lost Boys. They wanted to call the shots.

But God doesn't reward irresponsibility. And the truth is, neither do you and I. If a friend borrows money from you and then never pays you back, what will you say the next time he asks? If you find out that an acquaintance has shared something you said in confidence with someone else, will you trust her with your deepest, darkest secrets in the future? If your teenage son lies about where he's spending the evening, will you believe what he tells you about his plans for next weekend?

This isn't about forgiveness. Forgiving those who act irresponsibly toward us is our responsibility, no matter how difficult it proves to be. This is about holding each other accountable. That means being willing to take an honest look at the Peter Pan tendencies we hold in our own lives, not just pointing them out in others. Are you ready for a change of address?

CHAPTER 28

*I will not permit any man
to narrow and degrade my soul
by making me hate him.*

BOOKER T. WASHINGTON

SOMETHING POISONOUS GROWS IN THE WINTER OF OUR DISCONTENT

I t looked like a mansion out of a Hitchcock film. Weeds choked the path to the boarded front door. The windows were dark, an occasional pane covered with webs of cracked glass. The balcony looked ready to tumble at any minute. Even the gnarled trees that surrounded the former grand residence seemed to be bowed down with despair.

My Italian wasn't fluent by any means, having resided in Italy less than a year, but even I could interpret the sign above the door. It read *Villa Malcontenta*. House of Discontent. Who would name their house something like that? A pessimist, undoubtedly. But this house couldn't have always looked this way. Of course, with a name like *Malcontenta* it certainly seemed destined to wind up in exactly the state it was in. I wondered, if this villa had been christened "House of Joy" would things have turned out differently?

There's something in a name. Throughout the Bible people were given, or chose on their own, names that say something about their lives. In the book of Ruth, Naomi is a widow whose two sons have died, leaving her destitute with no family to support her through her old age. She changes her name to Mara, meaning bitter, because she feels that is the kind of life God has given her. In 1 Chronicles, a mother who suffered great pain in childbirth names her new baby Jabez. This name sounds like the Hebrew word for distress and pain. What a great legacy to pass on to a kid!

These days, unless you're a boy named Sue, like the one Johnny Cash sang about, your given name probably doesn't have all that much of an effect on your life. Most children's names are chosen for how they sound instead of for what they mean. But we often choose names for ourselves that we never speak aloud— loser, victim, disadvantaged, untalented, plain, unwanted, invisible, hopeless.

Sometimes we feel like Naomi. We believe that because of what's happened in our past, God has branded us with a name we never wanted. We wanted to be Happy, but we ended up as Grumpy or Dopey. It's not our fault. That's just our lot in life.

True, life is hard. And some people do seem to end up with much more than their fair share of heartache and pain. But not every one of these people choose to rename themselves Failure or Underdog. Why is that? It's because some people let bitterness grow in their lives, while others continually pull it up by the roots.

Hebrews 12:15 talks about how serious this problem really is. It warns us that when bitterness takes root, we miss out on experiencing God's gift of grace. We also have the ability to pass on that root to others, helping plant seeds of bitterness in the lives of those around us. We become a living, breathing *Villa Malcontenta,* our path to joy choked with weeds of resentment.

Pulling up roots of bitterness is not a weekend pastime. It's a lifelong battle. Any time we run into disappointment, sorrow, or pain, our hearts are fertile soil. The more we nurture those seeds by keeping a laundry list of grievances against others and complaining to anyone who will listen, the deeper the roots of our bitterness grow.

We've already discussed the importance of not comparing our lives to the lives of others and offering true forgiveness when we've been wronged. Those two steps are fundamental to uprooting bitterness. But without understanding and taking hold of God's grace, they won't take care of the whole problem.

None of us deserves the gift of grace. We can't earn it by being good and trying to do everything right. God offers it to us because He loves us. Grace allows us to see that God is working good out of every bad situation. It replaces resentment with thankfulness. It is the only thing that helps us rename ourselves with names like Blessed, Cherished, Beloved, and Victorious.

Bitterness blinds us to who God really is and who He has truly created us to be. Grace opens our eyes to promise and possibility. Just look at what happened to Naomi and Jabez. Naomi's daughter-in-law, Ruth, stood by her and ended up giving her another heir. Through Ruth, God blessed Naomi's life in ways she never thought possible. Jabez grew up to earn greater renown than all of his brothers. The reason? He asked God's guidance and blessing in making his life one that made a positive impact on those around him. Sometimes it's good not to live up to your name. Are there any names you've taken on that need to be changed?

CHAPTER 29

What lies behind us
and what lies before us
are small matters compared to
what lies within us.

RALPH WALDO EMERSON

FOR MATURE AUDIENCES ONLY . . .

The symphony of buzzes, chirps, and hums from the insects dwelling in the forest was like nature's alarm clock. My husband and preadolescent son awoke, listening quietly for a few moments to the racket that surrounded their cabin. "You know, Dad," my son commented, "all that noise is how some insects attract a mate."

Not wanting to miss a perfect opportunity for a conversation about the birds and the bees, my husband asked, "So, Ryan, how do you think humans attract a mate?"

My son thought for a moment, then replied with all seriousness, "They go to college!" My husband and I have endorsed that approach ever since.

However, the media would have us take a different approach. After all, who even needs a real mate? All we need is to attract someone to mate with. Monogamy is out. Promiscuity is in.

Today, anything and everything goes between mature, consenting adults. But being legally mature has little to do with emotional, spiritual, and mental maturity. And it has absolutely nothing to do with God's ideal of purity.

What does it mean to be pure in today's society? Isn't that just a ridiculously high standard that is out of step with the times? Haven't we matured beyond that kind of naiveté? Let's take a peek at the Webster's definition of "pure" to gain a little perspective: "Pure *(pyur)*: free from what . . . weakens or pollutes; containing nothing that does not properly belong; free from moral fault or guilt."

Wow. Purity actually sounds like a good thing, something beneficial, not just a criteria for prudish behavior. The truth is, God is not a sexual killjoy. In His eyes, sex is a good thing. After all, He designed it Himself. He created it as a mysterious, intimate bond between a husband and wife. Only when we take sex out of that context does it become something impure.

But impurity doesn't stop there. Even if we're physically following God's design, what we watch on TV or in the movie theater may prove that we're not as mature, or pure, as we think we are. The magazines we choose, the jokes we tell, and the comments we whisper under our breath reveal where our impurities lie.

Romans 12:2 tells us not to fit ourselves into the world's standards, but to be changed by renewing our minds. Sounds fairly simple. But how do we renew our minds? Is it like recharging a battery? Kind of. It's more like disconnecting ourselves from the lies of the world, then replugging ourselves into the source of truth.

Changing power sources isn't a gradual process. You can't unplug a light fixture from one socket and then hope as you get closer to the next socket that the light will become brighter and brighter. To renew your mind means that you have to actually remove yourself from one source before you can plug yourself into another one. This means plugging your life into a deeper relationship with God, time reading the Bible, a church that will challenge you toward living a pure life, and relationships that will help hold you accountable.

At the same time, you need to disconnect yourself from the things that are weakening or polluting your mind and your heart. To figure out what these influences are in your own life, take a tip from Philippians 4:8. Here we're told to think about whatever is true, noble, lovely, admirable, excellent, and worthy of praise. Would what you're doing, or viewing, fall into at least one of these categories? If not, it's time to unplug. Then, make the move to a power source that can actually change your life for the better. Now that's a sign of maturity!

CHAPTER 30

What you are is God's gift to you

and what you do with what you are

is your gift to God.

GEORGE FOSTER

"Good Enough" Never Is

Picture yourself on a tiny prop plane. The engine is so loud that conversation is out of the question. Your instructor helps you suit up with a parachute in preparation for your very first jump. You glance out the open door at the ground below. Fields, trees, cars, and houses seem so much farther away than you expected. Your heart begins to race. A little nervous, you try and joke with your instructor over the roar of the engine. "So you're a good parachute packer, right?"

"Good enough," he replies with a yawn as he pushes you through the open door . . .

When we pay others to fix our car, operate on our loved ones, or pack a parachute we'll soon be staking our life on, "good enough" is just not good enough. At least from our perspective. But when it comes to our own actions, where do we set our standards?

Living a life of mediocrity instead of a life of excellence has less to do with aptitude than with attitude. Take the life of Raoul Wallenberg. He was a Swedish diplomat during World War II. During the Holocaust, his position with the Swedish government afforded him a safe and privileged life. Wallenberg was a good diplomat, but that wasn't good enough.

Using his diplomatic connections, Wallenberg set up an office issuing fake passports for Hungarian Jews. But that still wasn't good enough. Wallenberg also set up housing, soup kitchens, and hospitals for the recipients of his bogus documents. But even that wasn't good enough.

On one occasion, Wallenberg saw Jews being loaded onto a train destined for the death camps. Instead of continuing to watch in safety, resting on the fact that he was already doing more than his part, Wallenberg demanded that all prisoners with passports be removed from the train. The prisoners began waving any piece of paper they could find, including driver's licenses, eyeglass prescriptions, and even deportation papers. He honored them all as passports, saving 300 Jews from a trip to the death camps that day. It is estimated that about 200,000 Hungarian Jews received diplomatic protection during the war, all because Raoul Wallenberg refused to live a life that was "good enough."

It's true that extreme situations present opportunities to go above and beyond the call of duty. But how about ordinary, everyday life? On the job, in your marriage, in your relationship with God . . . do you do just enough to get by? Life has a lot in common with all those classes you took back in high school and college. You get out of it what you put into it. A half-hearted effort will result in a half-lived life.

Mediocrity is certainly an attainable goal, but it's not very satisfying. So, why settle? The Latin phrase *carpe diem*—seize the day—is as true for us today as it was back in Roman times. The key is learning to be fully present wherever you are, whatever you're doing. That often involves limiting yourself to doing only one thing at a time. In this age of multi-tasking, driving a car while chatting on a cell phone and eating a burger may be considered using your time well. But what it's really doing is dividing your attention from the most important task at hand: safely maneuvering your car on the road.

What is your primary task at hand? If you've set aside time for a family vacation, ditch the pager, and don't call into the office. Focusing on your vacation will actually make it feel like one. And when you're at work, scrambling to get that last minute proposal to your boss, focus on that one task. Put your other projects aside until you've not only finished the hottest item on your list, but done it well. And if you want to really enjoy dinner, turn off the TV and actually take time to taste what you're eating.

Wherever you are, make sure you're all there. The past and the future are nice places to pay a brief mental visit to, but don't plan on living there. The present is your only current address. So invest in it. Do the best you can with this moment. Kiss mediocrity good-bye and welcome in challenge, opportunity, and possibility. You're "good enough" to handle it.

CHAPTER 31

You can discover more about a person

in an hour of play than in

a year of conversation.

PLATO

KID AT HEART, ELSEWHERE SLIGHTLY OLDER

O ur daily walk around the neighborhood was a tradition for my toddler son and I. As we walked, I'd tell stories about all of the things we'd see along the way. How blades of grass grow long like toenails so they need to be clipped with a lawn mower. How baby birds are hatched from eggs, but how his baby sister was growing inside of me. Why cats run away when Ryan would chase them with a stick.

When we arrived at a fire hydrant, I gave quite a detailed description on how the hydrant was filled with water so the firemen could use it to help us if our house ever caught on fire. Ryan walked up to the hydrant, which was just about his size, patted it on the "head" and yelled, "Hat!" Then Ryan gave its chain a hearty handshake and said emphatically, "Hi, Drant!" Obviously, something got a bit lost in the translation.

But after that day, I never looked at fire hydrants in quite the same way. They do look like squatty little men wearing hard hats. I'm glad I had a son who could help me see what was right before my eyes. Kids have a special talent for opening our eyes to the simple things we older folks have often forgotten along the way. They can find as much joy in a mud puddle as adults find in a new sports car. Obviously, kids have much to teach us grown-ups about getting the most out of life.

Is there a tiny teacher in your life? If you don't have children or grandchildren of your own, it's time to make friends with the neighbor kid. Babysit for friends. Volunteer to be a big brother or big sister. Not only will the kids you interact with benefit from spending time with you, you'll find yourself discovering a long lost art—the art of play.

Playing isn't wasting time. It's time well spent stimulating creativity, solidifying friendships, practicing teamwork, promoting exercise, and inspiring dreams. Can you remember how to enjoy yourself without the help of a remote control, amusement park, or cup of coffee? Kids can teach you how. They can show you how to lean back and find pictures in the clouds. They can demonstrate how a broken twig can be a fishing pole, bow and arrow, soup ladle, and conductor's baton, all in one. They can help you make friends on the playground, even if you don't know anyone by name. They can stop the aging process in your heart.

Even God tells us that kids have lots to teach us. In Matthew 18:1-4, He says that unless we become like little children, we won't enter heaven. Kids have faith in those bigger than they are. They trust what they say. They are not embarrassed to ask for help when they need it or to hug someone just because they feel like it. They fall asleep when they're tired, and they know that getting dirty isn't the end of the world. They say what they mean, cry when it hurts, and know how to have a good time without spending any money.

When was the last time you took a look at life from a kid's point of view?

The faster and more furious we go in life, the more we tend to view children as interruptions, instead of blessings—and teachers. So make a date with a child. Sit on the ground. Ask questions. Then listen to the answers. Watch kids play. Better yet, take off your shoes and hop in the sandbox with them. Remember, we've all got a long way to grow. God isn't finished with any of us yet, young or not so young.

CHAPTER 32

The envious praise

only that which they can surpass;

that which surpasses them,

they censure.

CHARLES CALEB COLTON

IT ONLY TAKES A SPARK TO KEEP A PERSON GROWING

M y little toes stick out. Other than the fact that this doesn't make me a candidate for a career in foot modeling, it also poses a problem. Every summer when I finally get to kick off those snow boots and enjoy the feel of the freshly mowed lawn under my bare feet, I'm faced with a challenge. Will I make it through the summer without breaking or spraining one of my little toes? If you were a gambling man, I'd give you odds of 50/50. Table legs and couch corners seem to be the main culprits. So every other summer I spend a few days hobbling around the house, a pained expression on my face, and a bulbous, purple, grape-like appendage protruding from the side of my foot.

Now logical people would say, "Why not just wear shoes?" The truth is, I've always been a barefoot kind of gal. So every summer I take the risk. But the truth remains. What sticks out gets broken more easily. Take car antennas, tree branches, and the arms (or lack thereof) on the statue of the Winged Venus. It's just a fact of life.

Believe it or not, that's good news for us as we mature. Proverbs 27:17 says that people can sharpen one another just like a piece of iron can sharpen another piece of iron. With the help of other people, we can work off those rough edges, smooth out the bumps, grind down those unsightly imperfections in our character.

We all have rough edges. We're not finished yet, remember? It would be nice if other people couldn't see our faults—our lumps and bumps. It would be more comfortable and much less humiliating. But it's actually a good thing that our faults rub others the wrong way. Sometimes we become so accustomed to our own flaws that we lose sight of them. It's only when those flaws grate on someone else that they come to light.

How well do you handle being sanded down by criticism? When iron sharpens iron, sparks fly. It's not a pleasant process. Feelings can get hurt along the way. But if you can quiet your pride long enough to listen, especially when the words come from a trusted friend, you might just learn something. If you go a step further and act on what you hear, you'll even mature a bit along the way.

However, criticism should be a buffing tool, not an instrument of torture. It's to help polish others, not cut out their hearts. Before you criticize someone, check your motives. Are you speaking out of love or just because that certain someone drives you nuts? Do you know that person well enough so that he or she will take your criticism constructively, or will your words produce all sparks and no change?

There will always be people in our lives who rub us the wrong way. My husband and I have nicknamed folks like these "porcupine people." They are hard to get close to without getting hurt. They don't just have a few rough edges. They're covered in quills. Some of them may exhibit these porcupine tendencies to everyone they meet, making them outcasts. Others may seem to save all of their quills for only you and me.

If you're the only one getting stuck, chances are there's an iron-sharpening-iron moment going on here. It's time to stop criticizing the other person and take a hard look at yourself. You may find a few quills sticking out of you.

If the other person truly is a bona fide porcupine, it's time to be a friend. Even if it's painful. Real love sees beyond the quills to the person-in-progress hiding underneath. With patience, encouragement, and a few carefully chosen words, you cannot only help another person mature, but sand down a few of your own sharp edges as well.

CHAPTER 33

Be glad of life because it gives you
the chance to love and to work and to play
and to look up at the stars.

HENRY VAN DYKE

LIFE'S TOO SHORT TO DO WHAT YOU HATE

When I was a little girl, I wanted to become a nun—and not just an ordinary nun. I wanted to be like the nuns who lived near my grandmother's house. They were members of a Carmelite order that had taken a vow of silence and poverty. All I knew was that they talked to God. I thought that sounded pretty cool.

Looking back on my childhood dream, I have to laugh. Not that choosing to become a nun is necessarily a bad thing. But the thought of me keeping my mouth shut and wearing the same thing every day sounds pretty impossible. Just ask any of my friends.

I also wanted to be a dancer. But my body leaned more toward a profession in sumo wrestling. Then there was that brief stint where I wanted to become a draftsman in the Navy. Luckily,

I spent some time talking to God. (I discovered I didn't have to become a nun to do that!) I realized that the one true passion I had throughout my life was writing. So that's the direction I headed. And I'm glad I did. Life's too short to spend it doing something you have no passion for.

Every week we have approximately 112 waking hours, of which most of us spend one-third to one-half on the job. That's a lot of time to do something you hate. But that's exactly what some of us are doing. Now there are always times in life when circumstances help choose our profession for us. When my husband and I were newly married and fairly destitute, we once took a job picking apples to help pay a phone bill. This was not my dream job. But at the time, it served its purpose.

Think back to when you were a kid. What did you dream of becoming? Are you doing anything that resembles those dreams? It's true that if every child who wanted to be an astronaut or a ballerina actually became one, we'd have a pretty unbalanced labor force. But that's no excuse for staying in a job you hate.

Why are you at the job you are right now? Do you consider it a profession, a vocation, or merely a necessary evil to help pay the rent? How does it fit in with your lifestyle and beliefs? Did you accept it based on the position's salary and benefits or how well it seemed to fit your own God-given talents and interests?

What is it, exactly, that gets you up and off to work over 2000 hours a year? It's been said that if you love your job, you'll never have to work a day in your life. My personal opinion is that any job, even one you love, will feel like drudgery on occasion. But if every day feels that way, it's time for a change.

That may mean a change in employment. It may mean figuring out how to get the education you need to qualify you for the job you want. It may mean taking a risk and moving to another part of the country. But it also may mean something even riskier. It may mean changing your heart, while your job description remains the same.

Colossians 3:23 says that we should work at everything we do with our whole heart, as if we're working for God, instead of people. Pride, greed, laziness, and apathy may have more to do with our lack of satisfaction at work than a poor job fit. Whatever the reason, it's time to take some action.

Work is not just something we do to pay the bills. It's a way to make a positive contribution to society. It's something that often serves other people and teaches us how to function together as a team. It's an activity that can help us understand our place in the world where we, and others, can benefit from the unique way God created each of us. Don't let complacency, or the hustle and bustle of the workweek, prevent you from taking a closer look at your job and your attitude toward it.

CHAPTER 34

God divided the hand into fingers

so that money could slip through.

MARTIN LUTHER

TO OWN OR NOT TO OWN . . . THAT'S A GOOD QUESTION

I t was a single blue eye. It watched me from its silent lair, unmoving, almost hidden in a sea of green ivy. But I knew it was there. All through lunch, I kept glancing its way and wondering. *What was that thing obscured in the landscaping of my friend's front yard?*

Finally, my curiosity got the best of me. I just had to ask. "Oh, that!" my friend replied. "It's a gift my mom got from my aunt awhile back." He pushed aside the leaves to reveal a terra cotta bird on a stake, stuck into the overgrown greenery. "None of us liked it, but it's out here just in case Aunt Celia drops by unannounced."

If you're like most Americans, you probably have the same thing. Not necessarily a bird on a stick, but trifles: gadgets you don't need, junk you don't want, things to dust and move and fix. You may even need a storage unit to hold it all. The question is, what are you going to do with it?

You may think that what you own has little to do with who you are. But, unfortunately, possessions take up more than just room in your house. They take up room in your heart. Take collecting things, for example. It doesn't matter if it's baseball cards or classic cars. Once you decide to start a collection, you've given yourself permission to buy everything you see that fits into that category. It's an investment, you tell yourself. But what are you and I investing in?

It feels like we're investing in our happiness. After all, it feels good to buy something, to be able to call it our own. But the more we become accustomed to buying whatever we want, the less we enjoy seeing what we cannot have. Just ask any true art connoisseur. The insatiable longing to own beauty can render a trip to a museum painful instead of fulfilling. All that beauty, inaccessible because it can't be owned. The same is true of a photographer. What happens when he sees the perfect sunset but has forgotten his camera? His experience of the sunset is bitter-sweet because he is unable to capture it on film and take it home with him.

This doesn't mean we're called to be monks, possessing nothing. It just means that we cannot let our possessions begin owning us. Matthew 6:21 tells us that wherever our treasure is, that is where our hearts will be found. What do you treasure? A good way to answer that question is by considering what you would try to rescue if your house were on fire. If your Porsche comes to mind before your family, that's not a good sign.

Loving *things* is not what love is for. God designed love to be shared in the context of relationship, not ownership. If things are taking up too much of your heart, you need to understand the emotions behind your purchases. Are you buying things to impress others, to fill a sense of emptiness within yourself, to improve your mood? Or perhaps you buy them just because you feel you deserve it? Things are meant to fill material needs, not emotional ones. Perhaps it's time to put a moratorium on spending, and deal with what's really going on in your heart.

And what about all of that other junk you own, but don't treasure: the broken toys, outdated clothing, and unwanted gifts? What about that terra cotta bird on a stick? Get rid of it. Throw out what's broken, and donate whatever is usable to a charitable organization. Just don't take it to the flea market. If today's trash once felt like a treasure to you, chances are you'll find yourself bringing home more stuff than you left with.

The less love that *things* take up in your heart, the more love you'll have to share with those around you and with God. Is it time you did a little spring cleaning?

CHAPTER 35

*Genius is 1 percent inspiration
and 99 percent perspiration.*

THOMAS EDISON

A Big Shot Is Only a Little Shot That Keeps Shooting!

ome people get all the breaks. They win the lottery. They're born with bodies that seem to discard calories like confetti—no matter how many chocolate truffles they consume. They always seem to be at just the right place at just the right time. It's easy to be a "big shot" if you've got luck on your side. But what about all of those "little shots" in this world? What about regular folks like you and me?

Never forget that the best strategy for a "little shot" who wants to become a "big shot" is to keep on keepin' on. Refuse to quit. Stay the course. Hang in there. NEVER GIVE UP!

After all, most "overnight" success stories are really written over a lifetime. Like any story, they can only be written one word at a time. Sound a little daunting? Most big shots-in-training would agree with you. Consider these fortunate few who *seemed* to have overnight success. Pulitzer Prize winning author Dr. Seuss received twenty-seven rejection notices for his first book. Thomas Edison filed more successful patents than anyone else in U.S. history—1,093, to be exact. He also filed 500-600 unsuccessful patents. What about that incandescent lightbulb that changed all of our lives? Edison tried over 6,000 different filaments before he discovered one that actually worked. That's practically the definition of "stick-to-itiveness!"

Failure is never certain until you've given up. But those mini-defeats along the road to success can be tough on your resolve. So how do you hang on in the meantime?

In a word—cheerleaders!

Whether it's writing the great American novel or losing five pounds, sharing your goals with those who believe in you can help you hang in there when the going gets tough. When selecting your personal cheering section, be sure to choose those who will celebrate your successes AND come alongside you when you have a setback AND ask how things are progressing along the way. Just don't neglect asking yourself the same question. If resentment begins to build every time your cheerleader asks how your goal is coming, chances are you're angry at yourself for doing nothing about reaching it. Even a cheerleader can't help an immovable object move forward.

That business about asking how things are progressing is really important on a personal level. Ask yourself how well you're doing at being your own cheerleader. Don't become a doomsayer and sabotage your own success. Unfortunately, that happens more often than we realize. We start off confidently and enthusiastically. Then as the challenges begin to appear, we gradually find ourselves trading in our "can do" attitude for a "can't do" mentality. Don't fall into that trap. Keep your eyes on what you've done right, not wrong. Look at how far you've come, not how far you have to go. Then celebrate every little victory along the way.

You know, there's Someone who's been cheering you on since the day you were born— GOD! In fact, He's your most adamant cheerleader. And not just after the fact. Many people ask Him for help once they've failed or remember to thank Him once they've succeeded, but they don't seem to understand that God wants to be a help and encouragement all along the way. Jeremiah 29:11 says that He has plans for your life—plans to prosper you and not to harm you, plans to give you a hope and a future. What a promise! And what a resource, especially when the going gets tough.

So when breaks just don't seem to be coming your way, do something about it. Refuse to give up! Persistence and determination will win out over luck any day.

CHAPTER 36

Anger is never without an argument,

but seldom with a good one.

GEORGE SAVILE, LORD HALIFAX

What's Cooking When You're Hot under the Collar

I remember the evening that our family's chicken dinner wound up on the ceiling. Those were the good old days. Back then, microwaves were still a sparkle in some inventor's eye. When Mom wanted to cook something more quickly than usual, she relied on a pressure cooker. But there was one hard and fast rule: Don't overfill it . . . or you'll wind up with chicken on the ceiling.

If you've never witnessed a pressure cooker blow, or haven't even heard of such an antiquated cooking device, you've undoubtedly missed out on some incredible pot roast. Cooking under pressure makes meat tantalizingly tender. Unfortunately, the same can't be said for people who rely on the pressure cooker approach to managing their anger. Their hearts seem to be anything but tender.

You know the people I'm talking about. They are the ones who blow without warning. They drive their cars, and use their tongues, like lethal weapons. With them, small things are never small. Apologies are always someone else's responsibility. They often blame their short fuse on the pressure they're under at the time. But they never seem to do anything to relieve that pressure or own up that the problem may lie within themselves, not just with the "jerks" they are forced to relate to in this world.

Along with the pressure cookers of the world, you'll also find the crock-pots. These are the people whose anger slowly simmers below the surface. From the outside, they may seem perfectly calm. But inside, even their ulcers are getting ulcers. You may not even know you've offended them. Those with crock-pot tendencies often hold hurt feelings, resentment, and even rage quietly inside. Their blood pressure, digestive system, and adrenal glands know what's going on. But the only clue those on the outside may have is when crock-pot folks stop talking to them or begin avoiding them altogether.

Would those who know you best say you err more on the side of a crock-pot or a pressure cooker? The problem with both of these approaches is that neither one takes an honest look at the heart of the problem—what is it that's pushing your hot buttons? Why, exactly, are you responding the way you are?

Figuring out what triggers anger is a little more complicated than it sounds. You may think it's "that lunatic who cut me off on the freeway" or "the fact that my son lied to me." But look deeper. Is the real trigger for your hot button your pride? Is it feelings of helplessness or not being able to control a situation or individual? The next time you feel a hot button being pushed, ask yourself, "What am I really afraid of?" Rejection? A loved one's safety? Looking incompetent? My own weakness or failure? Not being first?

Working out problems with other people is important. But until we get a handle on what's making us mad in the first place, our attempts at conflict resolution will do nothing more than put a band-aid on an infection that's bound to get worse. James 1:19

recommends that we be quick to listen, slow to speak, and slow to become angry. This involves more than thinking before we speak, once our hot buttons are pushed. This means taking time, before that happens, to actually disengage those hot buttons.

For both pressure cookers and crock-pots, the process is the same. It begins by asking God to reveal what's brewing inside us and why. If our anger is left unchecked, sooner or later there's going to be a mess. Pressure cookers may spew chicken on the ceiling, but crock-pots that are constantly on high will eventually bake on whatever's inside. Scrubbing off all that baked-on gunk is bound to be painful, even with God's help. With either approach, relationships are bound to be damaged along the way. So why wait any longer? Why not lift the lid and see what's heating up inside of you?

Chapter 37

If the world seems cold to you,

kindle fires to warm it.

LUCY LARCOM

It's Not Such a Small World After All

I f the world were your coloring book, how would you fill in the lines? Would the people all have white skin? Would you color them various shades of brown? Or would your world be "red and yellow, black and white," like the children we sing about who are precious in God's sight?

The truth is, our world has more color and variation than those extra large boxes of crayons I used to love to buy as a kid. There are no two people alike. We can lump them into race, nationality, age, even socioeconomic status. But all we are doing is grouping them, making generalizations. We are not seeing them for who they really are: individual works of art.

The more we get to know individuals who look and live differently from the way we do, the more we'll appreciate their beauty. But we humans like our niche. We like predictability and safety. We like to fit in. So we usually spend most of our time with people who bear a striking similarity to ourselves. It just feels more comfortable that way. Or does it just enable us to convince ourselves that we're superior?

Just imagine what it would be like if I said I loved art, but the only paintings I'd ever really seen were by Monet. Now Monet has done some magnificent impressionistic paintings. The colors, the texture, the feelings of serenity in some of his works from Giverny are truly masterpieces. But suppose another art lover brought over a Picasso from his own collection. My first reaction would probably be, "The colors are too garish! The angles, too sharp! It's just so loud! What's that thing supposed to be anyway? It's all mixed up! You call this ART?!?!?" Only by spending more time with the painting, by really looking at it, and perhaps learning about Picasso as a person, would I gain an appreciation for the artwork's own unique beauty.

That's why venturing out of our own little cultural box is important. It's hard to love what you fear. Prejudice is really the fear of what's different, what's unknown, what threatens to change the status quo we've grown accustomed to. A room filled with Monets may be nice for a while, but a museum filled with Van Goghs, Rembrandts, Pollacks, Picassos, and even artists no one has ever heard of before, is much more exciting. It helps us see the world through eyes that are different than our own. It stretches us. It helps us grow.

There are countless ways of gaining a broader world-view. Frequenting the occasional ethnic restaurant is a good start, but don't stop there. Watch the world news in addition to your local broadcast. Read a book written by an author from India or South America. Learn Turkish or French by listening to tapes during your morning commute. Find Bhutan on a map, then pray for the people who live there. Listen to world music CDs from Africa or the Caribbean. Rent a foreign film—with subtitles, if possible. Travel, whether in person or through videos or travelogues.

But don't just become a voyeur of foreign culture. Reach out to people outside your usual social circle. Make it a point to spark up conversations with people of other religions. Take part in a cultural celebration that is different from your own. Visit residents at a rest home. Host a foreign exchange student. Better yet, sponsor an impoverished child through an organization like Compassion International. Volunteer at an inner-city mission. If you have the time and energy, become a volunteer for the Red Cross.

Through it all, keep asking questions. Take time to understand what people believe about God, raising kids, world politics, and life in general. While on the outside our lifestyles, traditions, appearances, languages, and tastes in food may differ, inside we're all pretty much the same. We're all works of art still in progress.

—— ◯ ——

CHAPTER 38

Write injuries in sand,

kindness in marble.

FRENCH PROVERB

LOVE MEANS NEVER HAVING TO SAY YOU'RE SORRY . . . UNLESS, OF COURSE, YOU'VE DONE SOMETHING STUPID

We learn early in life that people are capable of doing mean things. Things that leave scabs on our knees and our hearts. Things that make kids cry and are hard to forget. Things we wish had never happened.

So we deduce that the world is divided into two kinds of people: mean people and nice people. Of course, this division is totally subjective. "Mean" and "nice" are determined by how someone treats us and our friends. Our judgments are quick and often final.

But as kids we also learn something about ourselves along the way. We learn that we have the power to be mean or nice, the power to hurt or help. When people are mean to us, we can pay them back. Of course, sometimes parents get in the way of this system. Especially when it's a sibling we've decided to get even with. Even today we can almost hear Mom say, her hands on her hips, "Now, tell each other you're sorry!" However, getting those words out is tough, even when what we're saying is an out-and-out lie. We're only sorry 'cause we got caught.

It really doesn't get any easier as we get older. Of course, we're not mean people. We're kind people just having a bad day. We know we should say we're sorry, but we certainly shouldn't have to accept all of the blame. We had our reasons. Or should I say, excuses?

Just think about how hard it is to say "I'm sorry" without adding a "but" right after it. "I'm sorry for getting mad, BUT you should have called." "I'm sorry I forgot to pick you up from school, BUT I got an important phone call." "I'm sorry for saying what I did, BUT you know that's a sensitive subject with me." "I'm sorry I spilled hot coffee all over the Johnson report, BUT I'm just not used to walking in these stilettos."

Whether we blame someone, or something, for our momentary lapse of kindness, or even cluelessness, the fact remains the same. We refuse to shoulder the blame for what we've done. We refuse to accept that we are responsible for our own actions.

Take a recent lawsuit I read about in the newspaper. The headline read, "Pop Tart Blamed for Fire." Why, that toaster pastry should serve life in prison for arson! What a menace to the American family! At least that's what the people who are attempting to sue the food manufacturer seem to be using as a defense. The truth is that they put the pastry in the toaster, then forgot about it and left the house. The pastry became lodged in the toaster and consequently caught fire. Imagine! A company not taking adequate measures to ensure that their food is non-flammable! Perhaps they should consider wrapping it in a little asbestos jacket. Oh, . . . sorry. That would undoubtedly bring about a lawsuit related to the dangers of asbestos.

Until we accept our responsibility for what we've done to hurt others, whether we did so intentionally or even inadvertently, any apologies that we manage to get out of our mouths will ring hollow. That goes for our apologies to God, as well.

Whom do you need to apologize to? Can you do it without any "ifs," "ands," or "buts"? Every time you voice those dreaded words, "I'm sorry," and shoulder your responsibility in the matter, regardless of what someone else has done, you take a step toward maturity. Your apology doesn't have to be accepted. That's someone else's responsibility. Just remember that humbling yourself to the point of asking another's forgiveness is not just being nice. It's the sign of an imperfect person choosing to love, and learn, instead of pass the blame.

CHAPTER 39

Nothing valuable can be lost

by taking time.

ABRAHAM LINCOLN

We May Be Going Nowhere, but We're Getting There Twice As Fast

When the truck in front of me hit the railroad tracks, I saw the unimaginable—an airborne rolltop desk. It had flown out of the truck bed like a newborn bird being pushed out of its nest. Only this bird had no idea how to fly. Instead, it fell to earth with the sickening sound of splintering wood.

Its honeyed finish, painstakingly sanded and stained, was now scratched and pitted from a collision with the asphalt. The gently curved rolltop lay to the east of the tracks. The drawers, to the west. So much for the countless hours I had worked between my job and college classes to finish my first real piece of furniture.

My friend, who had kindly offered to move my desk to my new apartment, was in tears. Strangely enough, I couldn't stop laughing. The words I'd read in Proverbs 23:4-5 that morning kept running through my head. They told me not to wear myself out working for money and the things it could buy because before I knew it they'd be gone. They'd sprout wings and fly away like an eagle. It was true. I'd seen it with my own two eyes. The eagle had landed.

I'd wanted a rolltop desk ever since I was a little girl. I figured I couldn't be a writer without one. So I'd worked and saved to make that dream come true. But somehow, when I saw those pieces of wood on the railroad tracks, I realized that's all it was: pieces of wood. Nothing of real consequence. Nothing of eternal value.

How much of our lives do we spend slaving away for things that don't last? Working overtime just to buy bigger toys? Running ourselves ragged to pad our investment portfolios? Sure, we enjoy a high standard of living compared to much of the world, when it comes to the size of our homes and the abundance of food in our pantry. But it seems that the higher our standard of living, the lower our satisfaction with life. The more conveniences we can afford, the less time we have to use them.

According to a recent study, Americans work more hours and take less vacation time than any other industrialized nation in the world. What for? An even higher standard of living? Not only are adults overworked, kids are starting to feel the stress as well. Where kids once enjoyed afternoons and weekends out playing at the park, they now spend time carpooling from one activity to the next. Their daily planners are as booked as their parents'. Aware of this growing trend, Girl Scouts can now earn a merit badge in stress management. Like mother, like daughter.

While acquiring more goodies is one motivation for over-work, filling an empty life is another. When life slows down, we actually have time to think. For some of us, having time on our hands takes us places we'd rather not go. But busyness is a great anesthesia. Don't want to deal with problems at home? Work late at the office. Feeling inadequate? Overachieve on the job, and you can rationalize away the need for relationships. Dealing with depression? Keep your *To Do* list full enough, and you can convince yourself, and others, that you're just overly tired.

Struggling with something God wants to change in your life? Crank up your commitments to the point where you've no time to listen to Him anymore.

How busy are you? Does your hectic schedule prevent you from getting together with friends, planning one-on-one time with your kids, volunteering in the community, spending time with God? Do you long for life to move at a slower pace—or are you afraid of what would happen to you if it did?

Your schedule is under your control, not the other way around. If your daytimer plays a bigger role in your life than your Bible, it's time to stop . . . and ask yourself why you're working so hard. Then ask God to help you take a fresh look at your priorities. Does how you spend your time really reflect what you believe is most important in life? If your life's stuck in the fast lane, it's time to get off at the nearest exit.

CHAPTER 40

The real voyage of discovery
consists not in seeking new landscapes
but in having new eyes.

MARCEL PROUST

WHEN THE PIZZERIA OF LIFE GIVES YOU ANCHOVIES . . . PICK 'EM OFF!

Life is filled with minor irritations. There's a detour on your way to work. A rock cracks your windshield. Your corned beef on rye ends up on wheat. The dryer quits. Your spouse forgets to pick up your dry cleaning. The kids outgrow yet another pair of shoes. You forget your PIN number. Then someone has the nerve to put the toilet paper roll on so that the paper rolls from the back, instead of the front.

How do you respond when you feel as though you've lived through an entire week of Mondays? Explode? Complain? Worry? Nag? Criticize? Wear an "Oh, woe is me!" pin on your lapel (or that same expression on your face)? Take it out on the person closest to you? Take it out on the dog? Take it out on God?

Why not just take that attitude out of your life? John 16:33 reminds us that in this life we will have trouble. If we expect things to always go our way, we're going to be more than disappointed. We're going to spend much of our lives as stressed out messes. It's true that our Constitution declares that we have an inalienable right to the pursuit of happiness. However, pursuing happiness doesn't mean we'll always catch up with it. If we get in the habit of bemoaning the little annoyances in life, chances are we'll miss out on the happiness we're so desperately pursuing. We'll also go over the edge when faced with a real crisis because we've been living so close to the edge the rest of the time.

What turns a small problem into a big one is often just a matter of perspective. Whatever is closest to us always looks larger than what may be off in the distance. Just ask a photographer. One finger left unwittingly in front of a camera lens can block out an entire mountain range. To put things into a realistic perspective, we need a reference point. That reference point comes with the second half of John 16:33. After God reminds us that we'll have trouble in this world, He tells us not to despair, because He has overcome this world. Our everyday annoyances look a lot smaller from the vantage point of heaven.

Stopping to ask our Heavenly Father for His perspective on our problems helps us sift the trivial from the important. It also helps us choose how we should handle a problem, instead of just instantly reacting to it. On the physical level, it helps us retrain that "fight or flight" instinct that gives our body a surge of adrenaline when we feel we're in danger. Constantly setting off that internal fire alarm is what often pushes anger, stress, anxiety, or depression into the danger zone.

In general, daily life is not one emergency after another. If it begins to feel that way, we need to look carefully at our own attitudes. Do we always have to be right? Do we have so much stuffed into our day that the slightest inconvenience sends our entire schedule into a tailspin? Do we take part in gossip that adds fuel to our emotional fires? Are our expectations of life and people unrealistic? Are we trying to control things that are ultimately only under God's control?

When it comes to problems that drive us nuts but are not a matter of life or death, we need to exercise our options of love, forgiveness, and patience. We need to choose to live life, not just react to it. Gaining God's perspective helps us do just that. It reminds us that individuals are more important than deadlines. Kindness is more valuable than our pride. Love doesn't hold a grudge. Today is a gift to celebrate, not a burden to carry.

But the choice is up to us. Will we let that lousy driver in front of us block out the beauty of the sunset overhead? Or will we let the Creator of that sunset help us see life, and our problems, through His eyes?

CHAPTER 41

Life is not a having and a getting,

but a being and a becoming.

MATTHEW ARNOLD

DON'T FOLLOW THE CROWD . . .
LEAD IT!

Remember the good old days when people were just trying to keep up with the Joneses? The Joneses were the people next door, the coworkers at our office, the folks in our community. Nowadays, the Jones family is obsolete. Today's culture whispers that we're expected to keep up with people we've never even met. People whose lives travel in seemingly different stratospheres. People in magazines and movies. People who spend their days shopping. People who dump their spouses like last year's fashions. People whose lifestyles we envy and emulate because they're rich and famous. What is their character like? Who knows? Who cares? All we know is that they sure look happy.

The media-crazed world we live in makes comparison seem so natural. We're surrounded by airbrushed images of what success looks like. It certainly doesn't live in an apartment, wear polyester, and work at the local convenience store. But for how many people is that life their reality?

The real problem with comparison is that it undermines contentment and self-esteem. Even if we use comparison to make ourselves feel better, by putting ourselves on a pedestal and looking down on others, we will end up with an inaccurate picture of who we are. God made only one of each of us. Comparing our bodies, our talents, and our life circumstances with anyone else is like comparing apples to oranges. It doesn't make sense.

But God tells us there is one area where we are encouraged to compare ourselves to one another. In 2 Corinthians 8:8 we are told to compare our love with the earnestness of those around us. This "love" can show itself in many ways. In this chapter of 2 Corinthians it talks about loving through giving. Giving isn't just donating to a local charity or putting your leftover change in the offering basket at church. Giving can be something monetary, but it can also be a gift of time, service, or prayer. It is any way that you give of yourself to help another.

How do you measure up? It all depends on whom you choose to compare yourself to. If you measure yourself alongside a murderer on death row, you'll probably feel pretty good about yourself. But if you measure yourself against someone like Mother Teresa, you may feel rather inadequate. But that's not the point of this type of comparison.

The purpose of comparing the earnestness of your love with another's is to inspire you; to encourage you toward giving more sacrificially. It's not a competition. It's more of a mutual admiration society. It helps you see how God can use anyone, and everyone, to make an impact on the world.

Let's go back to Mother Teresa for a moment. She was not blessed with wealth, athletic ability, or extraordinary physical beauty. She was not a powerful speaker or political leader. She was born to Albanian parents in Yugoslavia and became a nun at the age of eighteen. When she was thirty-six, she was stricken with tuberculosis. While recovering, she felt God wanted her to help the poorest of the poor; those who were not only over-looked but often despised and mistreated. Her ministry on the streets of Calcutta inspired Missionaries of Charity in Latin America, Africa, the Middle East, Australia, Asia, Europe, and even the inner cities of North America. In 1979, the earnestness of her love earned her the Nobel Peace Prize.

The small things Mother Teresa did with great love inspired others to give of their own lives more sacrificially. That is what God-centered, instead of self-centered, comparison can do. Could you use a little healthy comparison? Read biographies of men and women who've made a difference in our world. Ask others about what God has done in their lives to help them reach out in love. Then share your own story. What God has done through you might be just the inspiration that someone else needs to become all that God has created that person to be.

CHAPTER 42

One is not born into the world

to do everything but to do something.

HENRY DAVID THOREAU

There's Only One Savior of the World and (News Flash!) It Isn't You

I wanted to be neighborly. After all, my friend was only asking that I give up a night or two of sleep. On the sleep deprivation scale, she certainly ranked higher than I did. My baby and toddler had both worked into a regular nighttime routine several months earlier. But my neighbor's daughter was close to a year old and had still never slept through the night.

My friend explained that she was just too tenderhearted to let her baby cry. She'd run to her daughter's crib and pick her up at the slightest whimper. Since I'd done so well with my own kids, my neighbor felt that I was the perfect person to help train her baby to sleep through the night.

I had compassion for my friend and her daughter. I empathized with my neighbor's frustrations and lack of sleep. I listened to her share her struggles almost daily. I wanted to help out where I could. But I still said "no" to her request. It wasn't that I wasn't able to help. I could live without a little sleep. But what would happen when the kid needed to be potty trained? In other words, it was not my job to help that baby sleep through the night. It was her parents'. In certain recovery programs, doing someone else's job for them isn't considered loving. It's called enabling.

Parents are often the worst offenders. We want our kids' lives to be happy and pain free. We want them to mature, sure, but we don't want them to have to suffer along the way. Besides, we rationalize, it's just more expedient to do some things ourselves. So we do their laundry and clean their dirty dishes while they're parked in front of the television set. Helping a kid with his or her chores every so often is a favor. Doing them day in and day out gives kids the message that they are not really capable and that parents are merely servants awaiting their beck and call.

Some parents even shield their kids from the consequences of their own actions. They pay for the window that little Johnny broke. They convince the principal that little Sally didn't really mean to swear at the gym teacher and that staying after school would seriously disrupt her ballet lessons. Later on, they bail their kids out of jail, buy them new cars when they wreck the old ones, and let them move back home when they are struggling financially. Helping out in this way is not always bad. But if what we do for our kids reinforces reckless, irresponsible behavior, we're not saving them any pain. We're just delaying it. Sometimes with disastrous results.

And it's not just our kids who we try to save. It could be the needy family down the street. Helping them once may be servanthood. Helping them twice may be kind. Helping them three times may teach them that they have no need to help themselves. Our efforts can look so altruistic and innocent. We may buy gifts we can't afford for friends who are feeling down. We may listen to people's sad stories over and over again without having the courage to confront them on their own shortcomings. We may drop everything to run and help a neighbor when our own family is desperately in need of our time or attention.

"Love one another" does not equal "save one another." Not only is it impossible for us physically, it simply isn't our job. Sometimes brokenness, disappointment, and even despair are the tools God uses to help people mature. Other times, God may have someone else in mind to fill a need. Our overzealous efforts, often born out of a need to feel needed, instead of honest-to-goodness love, may actually teach others to turn to us before they turn to God. Talk about shoes we were never meant to fill.

So the next time you're ready to swoop in and rescue someone, take a moment to ask yourself a few questions. Is this problem a natural consequence this person needs to learn from? Am I the person who should be meeting this need? Is love motivating me toward action, or is it the desire to feel admired or needed? Will my actions lead this person toward, or away from, God?

If you feel God giving you the go-ahead, by all means don't hesitate. Just remember that He's the only One who can do it all.

CHAPTER 43

Preach the gospel at all times.

If necessary, use words.

ST. FRANCIS OF ASSISI

Some Bibles Have Legs instead of Pages

———⟨∽⟩———

The British press called Eric Liddell "a traitor to Scottish sporting." After all, Liddell was favored to win the first Olympic medal in track and field that Scotland had ever been in contention for. But the qualifying heat for the 100-meter race in the 1924 Olympic games was scheduled to take place on a Sunday. Liddell believed that Sunday was a day to give God glory, not to earn it for yourself. So as the shot from the starting pistol rang out Sunday morning, Liddell was not at the track. Instead, he was preaching in a church nearby.

But Liddell's most powerful sermon wasn't the one he gave from the pulpit. It was the one he lived out day by day. Though the "Flying Scotsman" went on to win an unexpected gold as he set a new world record in the 400-meter race, as well as placing third in the 200-meter, it wasn't only his speed that won Liddell notoriety. It was his commitment to honor God.

Not everyone reads the Bible. But if you believe in God, people are constantly reading you. What message are you sending them? You may not hold the same convictions about running on Sunday that Liddell did, but what convictions do you hold? Do you believe people are of value to God? Do you believe God has asked you to be honest in your business practices? Do you believe that serving others is a way to share God's love? Do you believe that there is life after death?

Whatever our true convictions are will be evident in the way we live our lives. Suppose I say that I believe that physical fitness is a necessity in my life. But suppose I also subsist on Dr. Pepper and donuts. I haven't had a check-up with my family doctor since I went to summer camp in junior high. And the only consistent exercise program I participate in is raising the footrest on my recliner before I plop myself down to watch my daily four hours of television. Would you say that I really believe in the importance of physical fitness? My lifestyle would lead you to come to a totally different conclusion about my convictions in this area.

Living a life based on our convictions is more than practicing what we preach. It's recognizing that if we say one thing but do another, we're fooling ourselves about what we really believe. Those around us, however, don't seem to be fooled quite so easily.

What do you suppose your neighbors would say if they were asked about the convictions you hold? How about your coworkers? Your children? Those who happen to be driving near you? If you believe that God is at work in your life, your actions should reflect that fact.

Does your life look any different from the lives of those around you who don't believe in God? Eric Liddell's did. Not everyone agreed with his decision. Some people criticized him. Others probably thought him a fool. But in God's eyes, he was a man of honor. His convictions eventually led him far away from the fame of the Olympics to become a missionary to China, like his father. Where will your convictions lead you?

Your life will tell a different "Bible story" than anyone else's. You may end up as a missionary in China. Or you may wind up as an art teacher in Burbank. You may preach to packed auditoriums about what God has done in your life. Or you may serve quietly in the background of your kid's kindergarten classroom. Whatever you do, the convictions you hold will preach a more convincing sermon than anything you'll ever say. Will that sermon be one that draws others to God or away from Him?

—— ◯ ——

CHAPTER 44

Forgiveness is the fragrance that the flower

leaves on the heel of the one who crushed it.

MARK TWAIN

When Life Hurts, Don't Pick at the Scab

others are a never-ending source of advice. Regardless of language or millennia, you can hear their words repeated through the ages: "Put that down or you'll poke your eye out!" "Eat your vegetables or no dessert!" "Put it back where you found it!" "If you cross your eyes, they'll stay that way!" "Wear clean underwear in case you're hit by a car!" (car being interchangeable with chariot, wagon train, rickshaw, or ox cart), and "Don't pick at the scab, or it'll never heal!"

Sometimes mother does know best. But as every kid knows, listening to advice is one thing. Following it is quite another. Especially when it comes to scabs. They're just so . . . interesting. They keep changing, like a battle scar turned chameleon. If you're bored, they're a portable science project inviting you to experiment. But it's true, the more you pick at the wound, the longer it takes to heal.

The same thing holds for wounds of the heart: being chosen last on the softball team, watching someone you love breathe her last breath, suffering abuse at the hands of a troubled parent, being abandoned by your spouse. These wounds take time to heal. But the good news is, they do heal—if we let them.

A wound of the heart needs to be treated in much the same manner as a skinned knee. First the wound needs to be cleaned. I still remember my mom's words as she grabbed that bottle of hydrogen peroxide from the medicine cabinet to deal with my playground spills: "This is going to sting a little." That was always an understatement. The deeper the wound, the greater the sting of cleaning it out.

Cleaning a wound of the heart isn't pleasant. It may involve talking things out with the one who hurt you or making an appointment with a trustworthy counselor. It most certainly will include telling the Great Physician just where it hurts, and why. You can choose to skip this step. You can hide your wound or ignore it altogether. Unfortunately, unattended wounds are prone to infection. You may think you've buried the pain, only to have it fester into an even greater problem further down the road.

Time, by itself, does not heal all wounds. We need to take action. So after cleaning the wound, we need to choose to cover it with the proper bandage: forgiveness.

"No way!" I can hear you say. "You don't know how deep this wound is! I refuse to forgive and forget." God never told us we had to forget what has happened. He simply told us we need to forgive. Forgiveness is not making excuses for what someone else has said or done that has hurt you. It's not making the offense seem smaller or just pretending it never happened at all. To really forgive someone, you need to be honest about how much you've been hurt. You need to acknowledge how deep your wound really goes. Only then can you choose to offer forgiveness; not because the person who hurt you deserves it, but because it's the right thing to do. Relationships, and your own heart, cannot heal without it.

Another good thing about a bandage is that it helps deter us from trying to pick at the scab. As deeply emotional wounds start to heal, we sometimes have that urge to check and see if they still hurt. We relive the offense in our minds or recite it in detail to those around us. We may even feel the need to show off the wound to others as a badge of our bravery or to gain sympathy. Some of this is natural in the process of healing, but if it continues after we've put on that bandage of forgiveness, there may be a problem. Just like Mom said, continuing to pick at it will slow down the healing process.

This doesn't mean we should never share our battle scars with others. Sharing how God has helped us heal from deep wounds in our lives can be encouraging to those who are just beginning to clean out their own. But the key is sharing to facilitate healing, not to play "my scab's bigger than your scab!"

When we're injured, we dedicate much of our energy toward recovery. Only after we're feeling better do we move forward. Taking proper care of the wounds receive in life will help get us back on the path to maturity as quickly as possible.

CHAPTER 45

The pessimist sees difficulty in every opportunity.

The optimist sees opportunity in every difficulty.

WINSTON CHURCHILL

THE BREAD DOESN'T ALWAYS LAND JELLY-SIDE DOWN

———⟨∼⟩———

I was running errands when the tire went flat. It wasn't one of those nice slow leaks where you noticed the tire was getting a bit squishy and had plenty of time to limp the car to the nearest mechanic. It was a boom-splat-come-to-an-instant-standstill type of flat. My girlfriend and I hopped out of the car and surveyed the damage. "Flat as a pancake," as my grandmother used to say in Polish when I was a child. This tire wasn't taking us anywhere.

I thought back to my high school days when I had learned how to change a tire in driver's training. Several decades had passed since then. Never having the opportunity to put my knowledge to use, it had long since faded away. I vaguely remembered something about a jack and loosening the lug nuts in a criss-cross fashion. We were doomed.

Then a cowboy in a white hat strode across the parking lot. At least he could have been. From where my girlfriend and I were standing, the guy looked like a hero. Actually he was a salesman from the men's store we'd awkwardly parked in front of. With a warm smile, despite the snowflakes that were starting to fall, Bob offered his help.

After I admitted I had no idea where the tire iron or jack were, Bob knew the situation was more desperate than he had first thought. Rising to the challenge, Bob and a few other employees rigged a jack designed for a Honda to work on the body of my four-wheel-drive Bronco. Crawling under the Bronco in his perfectly pressed pinstripe suit, Bob proceeded to get the flat tire off of the car and put the spare in its place.

During this process, a winter storm began to blow violently across the parking lot. Where an hour before my girlfriend and I were enjoying a bit of springtime in the Rockies, now winter returned with full force. Being as prepared for a change in weather as I was for changing a tire, I had not even thrown a jacket in the car that morning. But if Bob were lying in his suit on a piece of cardboard on asphalt that was slowly turning white with snow, I could certainly stand by his side guarding the lug nuts from the gale force winds that threatened to knock the car off the jack.

After the less-than-adequate spare was in place, Bob encouraged me to head to the nearest mechanic and get a real tire on my car. Refusing any kind of compensation except profuse thanks, Bob hurried back into work as my girlfriend and I watched. It was the first time I remember seeing an angel wearing a three-piece suit.

Unfortunately, our next stop at the mechanic's was not quite so inspiring. Replacing the tire was not a problem. Repairing the four-wheel drive hub that Bob had damaged while changing the tire was of greater concern. And discovering the AAA card in my wallet that promised free assistance in case of a flat just added fuel to the fire.

But what amazed us was that there was no fire. It's true, the day seemed like a comedy of errors. But better that than a tragedy of despair. It's not that we are perpetual optimists. It's just that the blessings of the day seemed to outweigh the inconveniences. The tire went flat in a parking lot, not on the freeway. I wasn't alone when it happened. A hero came to our rescue. We didn't have any pressing appointments that we weren't able to fulfill. The expense wasn't something I'd planned on, but it wasn't going to put me on the bread line either. I relearned how to change a tire and how NOT to crack a four-wheel drive hub. And the sun shining through clouds filled with snow was really beautiful, despite the cold. All in all, I chalked the day up to experience and the joy of making a new friend at a men's clothing store. That's a lot more exciting than anything I had planned.

Life is a grindstone. Everything from minor inconveniences to heartbreaking tragedies rub against us from birth to death. But our attitudes determine whether the events along the way grind us down to nothing or polish us into something beautiful. Which way will you view the daily grind today?

Chapter 46

Love is never lost.
If not reciprocated it will flow back
and soften and purify the heart.

WASHINGTON IRVING

NEVER MISS A CHANCE TO SAY "I LOVE YOU"

Mark's dorm room was a masterpiece. Seventy-two construction paper hearts decorated his walls, each inscribed with a different reason why I loved him. A large heart-shaped chocolate chip cookie, his favorite, was propped against his pillow. His Valentine's Day gift was complete. Mark and I had only known each other a few months, but one thing was certain. Somewhere down the road, we were getting married.

When Mark opened the door to his room, he was more than surprised. And it was not just my creativity, hard work, and sentiment that made him feel that way. The truth was that he'd forgotten it was Valentine's Day. He hadn't even bought a card.

Welcome to the real world of love and romance. Most days it bears little resemblance to the kind of passion and devotion portrayed in the movies. In real life, love is hard work. Just look at 1 Corinthians 13. It gives us a picture of what genuine love looks like: patient and kind, not jealous or boastful or proud or rude, doesn't demand its own way, isn't irritable, keeps no record of wrongs, doesn't delight in evil, rejoices in the truth, always protects, always trusts, always hopes, never gives up—love never fails.

Always and never—those are tough words to live up to. As we read this list, it's so easy to see where the people close to us fall short—our spouses, kids, parents, best friends. (What's that part again about keeping no record of wrongs?) What's harder to accept is how far off our own love is from this picture.

The good news is that God isn't finished with our love any more than He's finished with any other area of our lives. Our love, like our lives, is a work in progress. So are our relationships. It's easy to give 1 Corinthians 13 kind of love when we're head over heels and the object of our affection seems to do no wrong. But what happens when love isn't convenient? When it gets its feelings hurt? When those warm, fuzzy emotions are nowhere to be found? When it's ignored or even betrayed?

Love is a verb. It's a deliberate action, not a reaction. As in every area of our lives, we have a choice whether we will love someone or not.

When relationships are rocky, this choice is obvious to us. Unfortunately, when things are going smoothly, love faces an enemy that looms just as large: complacency. We take the people we love for granted. We treat them as though they'll always be there. We get in the habit of making our own success and fulfillment a higher priority than our relationships. And then we wonder why we feel so alone.

Love grows best when it's expressed. If you care about someone, don't keep it a secret. Kiss your wife, just because. Tell your kids how lucky you are that God entrusted them to you. Drop your best friend a card, even if she lives right next door. Call your mom just to ask how she's doing, then really listen to what she says. Make big deals out of birthdays and anniversaries. And yes, even Valentine's Days.

Our love story didn't end that February over twenty years ago. But Mark never forgot Valentine's Day again. Two years ago, he even surprised me by saying I had an hour to pack for an undisclosed destination. We hopped on a plane and ended up in San Antonio, Texas—just because it was a place I'd mentioned that I'd love to visit sometime.

Love listens, apologizes, forgives, surprises, celebrates—even fails sometimes. At least in this life. But love never gives up. Only God's love for us will always look like 1 Corinthians 13. But He's a great Teacher. What love lessons does He have in store for you today?

CHAPTER 47

Fear knocked at the door.

Faith answered.

And lo, no one was there.

A N O N Y M O U S

LIONS AND TIGERS AND SCARES . . .
OH, MY!

———⌐∽⌐———

Every night it was the same scenario. I tried not to look at my closet door. But like a spectator drawn to the scene of an accident, I couldn't seem to stop myself. And every night it was still there. The face of a witch in the grain of the wood. Even into my early teen years, I'd pull the blankets up over my head to help relieve my fears and try to lull me to sleep— with limited success.

Fear can make us do some pretty crazy things. We whistle in the dark, hold onto our lucky rabbit's foot, or check under our beds for monsters. When I was in seventh grade, during the height of my wood-grain phobia, I wrote a catchy little ditty: "If you were really very scared, but you just kept on going, don't you think there might just be a little bravery showing?" I won a seventh grade poetry contest with those simple words. But at that time, I knew that courage was not an attribute I seemed to possess. I would just as soon run the other way.

As kids we often have some pretty irrational fears. But how about as adults? Have we really changed? We may no longer believe in the boogie man, but fear can still stop us dead in our tracks. The fear of the unknown can prevent us from getting married, having kids, or changing jobs. The fear of being known can keep us paralyzed with embarrassment, shame, or the feeling that we just don't measure up. It can keep us living our lives as though we still had the covers over our heads.

Not that fear can't also be a good thing. Fear puts our adrenaline into high gear so we can run away from danger. It heightens our senses and makes us more alert when running away is not an option. It is also the stimulus that ignites true courage and bravery under extraordinary circumstances.

Our fears can also help enlighten us as to what areas of our lives need some serious attention—what areas God isn't finished with yet. However, fear that seems out of proportion to the danger we face is a warning sign that something inside of us is out of balance. The absence of fear may be just as serious a warning sign. People who take unnecessary risks—repeatedly doing things to jeopardize their jobs, their relationships, or their health—are not courageous. They are simply living in denial.

So much of life gives the illusion that we are in control. We get an education, work hard, save our money, buckle our seatbelts, and lock our doors. We feel secure. But all it takes is an unexpected calamity to shatter that illusion—a diagnosis of cancer, a fire that destroys our home, a spouse that confesses to an illicit affair. All of a sudden, we're reminded how little control we really have over life. Fear is born out of the knowledge that, ultimately, we are not in control. In that sense, fear only exposes the truth: we are not God.

But fear can do something beyond exposing our weaknesses or awakening courage we never knew we had. Fear can also draw us closer to God. Whether it is facing impending danger, just dealing with something that makes us vaguely uncomfortable, or becoming irrationally paralyzed by a situation that leaves us feeling phobic, God's presence is as close as our fear.

Life is fragile on this earth. There are things that spark fear in us. But we never have to face those fears alone. God is there, and He's in control. Of course, if He's in control, why does He let some of the things we're afraid of actually happen? That, my friend, is another chapter.

CHAPTER 48

He who has a Why to live for

can bear almost any How.

FRIEDRICH NIETZSCHE

WHY PINOCCHIO LONGED
TO BE A REAL BOY

D o you remember how to play "let's pretend"? As a kid, it was easy. One minute you could be a fireman, the next an astronaut, or even the ruler of a fairy tale kingdom. But let's try something a little different. Let's pretend you are God. It shouldn't be too hard. After all, most of us live our lives as though that were true much of the time. But for just a moment, let's pretend that you are creating the world. You've made light and dark, some incredible stars, planets, and solar systems. You've really enjoyed yourself by creating animals of all kinds, from aardvarks to porcupines. You've fashioned sunsets and mountain ranges, fruit trees and rose bushes. But there's something missing. Someone to interact with. Someone to love.

Now you could create your very own action figure. You could change its clothes, pose it in all sorts of lifelike positions, and pretend to have some stimulating conversations. Or you could create a friend—someone who breathes and moves on his own, someone who can learn and grow, someone who can actually love you back. Which would you choose?

The answer seems simple. But the consequences of that decision are not. Once you create a person, instead of a toy, the problem of free will comes into play. What if that person chooses not to love you? What if that person chooses to hurt others that you love? Let's face it. An action figure would be much safer. But what kind of relationship can you have with a mere puppet?

Whether or not a good God can allow evil things to happen presents a question that the wise have debated for centuries. So why bother with it here? Does it really belong in a book on how to mature into a better person? Actually, that question is at the heart of what we're talking about. If God is not in control, or if He does not have our best interests in mind, why would we even want God to help "finish" us? Would He be worthy of such an important job? Is life really just a self-help program? Or does a loving God play an integral part, even when He allows bad things to happen?

A few short pages is certainly not going to fully answer this question. But just ignoring it won't help out much, either. We all need to find an answer to this question before we can trust God to really work in our lives. The God we've read about in the Bible, the One who's answered our prayers and helped change our hearts, certainly seems capable enough, powerful enough, wise enough to be in control. But how much control does He really exercise in the world?

The picture of God as a Father is a good one. He participates in the birth of His children. He teaches them, provides for them, gives them guidance, advice, and blessings. But He also lets them fail. Sometimes His children make Him proud. Other times His heart is broken. He continues to love them, but He won't force them to go a way their hearts refuse to go. That would be slavery, not parenthood.

Romans 8:28 reminds us that God can bring good out of any situation. Of course, God's idea of good may differ a bit from our own. A diet of donuts may be a kid's idea of what's good, but a wise parent will be sure to work in those vegetables to ensure a healthy balance. A smooth, shiny knife may look like a good toy to a toddler. But a loving parent will keep knives out of a child's reach, no matter how loudly the child cries and whines about how much he wants it. That's why some of our prayers don't receive the answers we'd hoped for. God is just being a good parent.

As a good parent, God works everything in our lives toward our ultimate good—even the bad stuff. How would we learn patience if we got everything we wanted right away? How would we learn sacrifice if our needs always came first? How would we learn what real love is if we lived in a world full of puppets?

Okay. Time to stop pretending you're God. It's time to start looking for the reasons you're glad God has the job, instead of you. Then, why not make a list of how God has brought about good through difficult situations in your life. The next time you're faced with that question of why God would allow something like this to happen, read your list. Then thank God you're so much more than a puppet. You're a beloved child.

CHAPTER 49

God loves each of us

as if there were only one of us.

ST. AUGUSTINE

IT'S NOT WHAT YOU DO, IT'S WHO YOU ARE

I'm living proof that God doesn't answer prayer. Well, one prayer I've prayed, anyway. And it's a biggee. I have a mouth that doesn't know when to quit. Sometimes it complains, gossips, tells off-color jokes, and puts others down. I've prayed that God would fix this problem of mine, that He'd finish this area of my life. But so far, He's said "no." Not that I haven't made any progress. I have. But it's slow and uneven. And I'm thankful.

Okay, so now you're really confused. But the truth is, if I suddenly had my mouth under control, other people might think I were perfect. Well, at least in that area. That would be incredibly far from the truth. You see, the only reason I really wanted God to clean up my speech was so that others wouldn't see what was really going on in my heart. But if it were easy for me to hold my tongue, while my attitudes remained the same, this answered prayer could actually be a curse. I could sound kind, compassionate, and mature, while remaining critical, crass, and ungrateful.

What matters most—how I appear to others or who I really am? For us people-pleasers, that can be a tough question to answer. But when it comes to how God views the problem, the response is clear: It's not what we do; it's who we are.

In a book like this, that concept may not always be clear. After all, there are so many things we need to do to mature. Forgive. Apologize. Take responsibility. Don't procrastinate. Be honest. Reach out to others. Keep learning. Deal with our fears. Slow down. Apologize. Pray . . . It begins to feel as though life is just a test to see if we're getting more and more things right.

If it's true that God is never really finished with us, is it even possible to reach our potential? After all, the deeper we look into our hearts, the more we find that needs changing. That doesn't make for great motivation. It sounds like we're running a race that can never be won.

We must remember Who is in charge of the race. God isn't standing at the finish line to see who comes across it first. He is running right alongside each of us. Even when He has to run slowly. Think back to what we learned about grace earlier. In God's eyes, we've already won the race He's set before us. His love for us has nothing to do with our performance. Like a proud parent, God is cheering for each of His children, no matter where they are on the track.

All of the things I've encouraged you to do throughout this book, like serving others, being more generous with your time and money, or working on becoming more patient or less angry, are all good things. But our goal is not to become better people, though that's a great side benefit. Our real goal is to live a deeper life spent closer to God.

Our God-given potential isn't so much a standard that we're trying to live up to, as it is a pair of shoes we're growing into. The trick is, that shoe size changes every day. What we learned yesterday helps determine what our potential for today looks like.

Some of our biggest victories may not even be apparent to anyone but God and ourselves. But we're not running this race for the applause of those around us, remember?

So let's put on the shoes that fit us today, and run the race that's set before us right now. Forget the skinned knee from yesterday. Don't focus on the finish line forty years down the road. Just keep your eyes on what God's set right in front of you. Then, don't forget Who's running beside you, cheering you on every step of the way.

CHAPTER 50

Life is the childhood of our immortality.

GOETHE

THE END, SORT OF . . .

Once a year we celebrate the anniversary of our birth. Even if others forget our special day, it's not a date that slips our own minds too easily. But there is another anniversary that passes by each year unnoticed. That is the anniversary of the day we will die. Though the date remains a mystery, except to God, how we view that day plays a part in how we live our lives.

Would knowing that date change how you spend today? If you knew you still had fifty years ahead of you, would you relax a bit more? Or would you work harder than ever, trying to save enough money to help you make it financially? Would you take those piano lessons you've always wanted? Or would you put them off, knowing you've still got time?

And what if you discovered that the date of your death was tomorrow? Chances are you wouldn't spend today at the office or cleaning house. You'd leave your *To Do* list unfinished, the dishes unwashed, and gather all the people you love around you to tell them how much they mean to you. You'd savor the beauty of the sunset. You'd enjoy the taste of each meal. You'd be more aware of the passage of time. You'd make every minute count.

Tomorrow may be the day. But then again, you may have fifty years. To be lost in either extreme is to lose sight of the whole story. The key is to learn to live a life that balances both possibilities at the same time. Seize today, while planning for tomorrow. But don't let death convince you it's the final chapter. God isn't finished with you yet . . .

Though your story on earth may have ended, eternity has just begun. Though what it will really be like is still a mystery, there are clues. God has promised not once, not twice, but three times (Isaiah 65:17, 2 Peter 3:13, and Revelations 21:1) that there will be a "new heaven and a new earth." To me, that's synonymous with adventure. If God's first Grand Canyon was merely grand, imagine what He could do the second time around!

God has also said we'll be given new bodies (1 Corinthians 15:51-52). The blind will see. The lame will walk. The tone deaf will sing. The uncoordinated will dance. We'll have bodies that will work all the time—ones that will never grow old and die, ones we'll not need to compare to those around us.

Best of all, there will be relationship. After all, relationship is the ultimate story. It is never static. In relationship there is growth and change and love and discovery. But in heaven, God has also promised in Revelation, there will be no more tears. (See Revelation 7:17 and 21:4.) Can you imagine the joy of being in a relationship that never gives you cause to cry? A relationship where there is always more than enough time to get to know each other better?

The relationship that you begin on earth with God is just a prelude—the "foreword" of your life's story, so to speak. Though it seems brief in light of eternity, there is something about our lives here on earth that matters deeply to God, and should to us, as well. Everything we do and say either draws us closer to God and others or further away from them. Our actions either bless others or hurt them. They either perfect us or degrade us. While each of us is a work in progress who still blows it along the way, maturing means learning from our mistakes—and letting God change us from the inside out.

Heaven truly is something worth looking forward to. And death, while unsettling in its unpredictability, is not to be feared. God is there. From the first spark of life in your mother's womb, through the mystery of death and into the never-ending story of eternity, you're never alone. God is beside you, loving you and helping you grow. So be patient with yourself and others. God not only isn't finished with us yet. The truth is, He never will be.

Additional copies of this book
are available from your local bookstore.

If you have enjoyed this book, or if it has impacted your life,
we would like to hear from you.

Please contact us at:

Honor Books

Department E

P.O. Box 55388

Tulsa, Oklahoma 74155

Or by e-mail at *info@honorbooks.com*